THE POWER OF VENUS

SONIA MUTHURAJ

ILLUSTRATED BY AYRA AJAY

Halo
PUBLISHING
INTERNATIONAL

ISBN: 978-1-63765-111-7
LCCN: 2021917697

Halo Publishing International, LLC
www.halopublishing.com

Printed and bound in the United States of America

To my two amazing grandmothers, who were
the first to show me the true power of Venus.

PART 1:

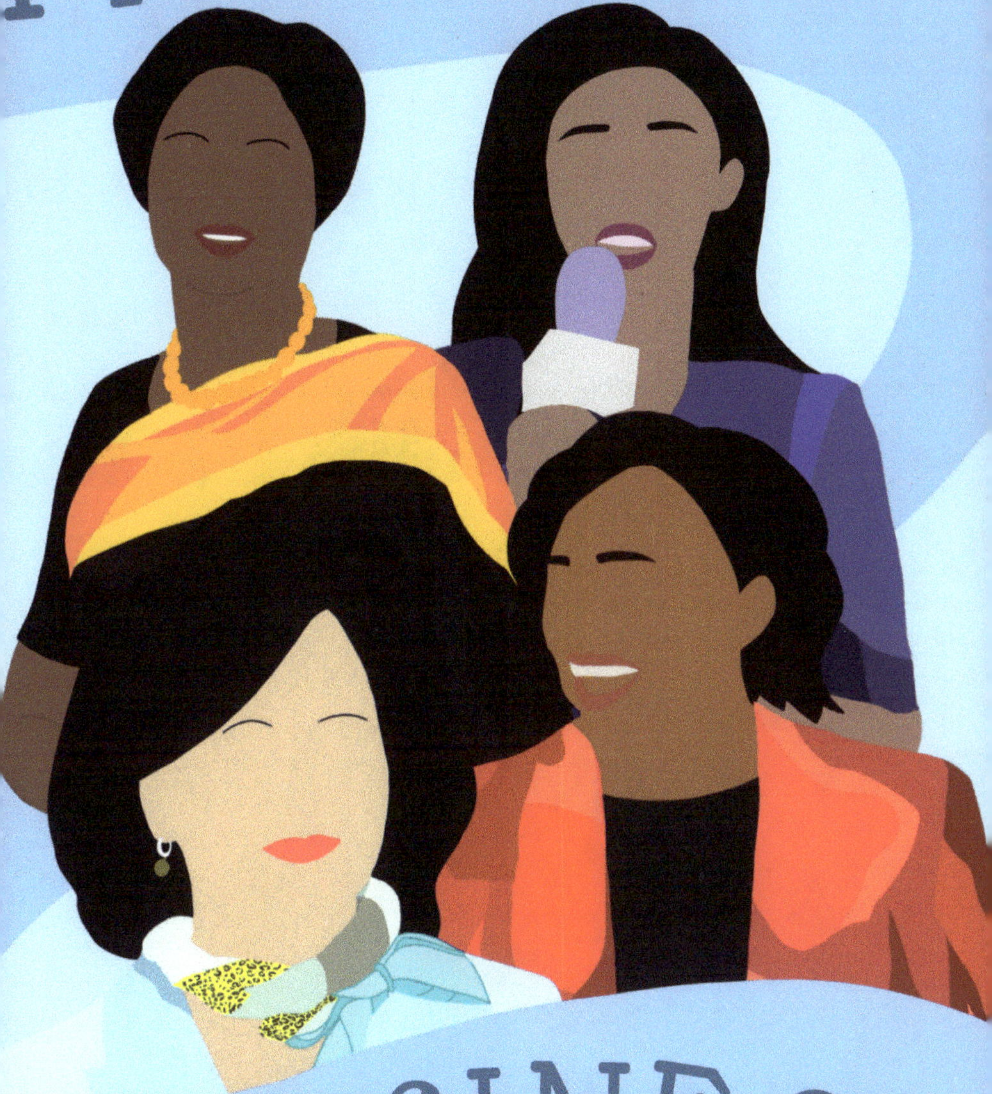

BUSINESS

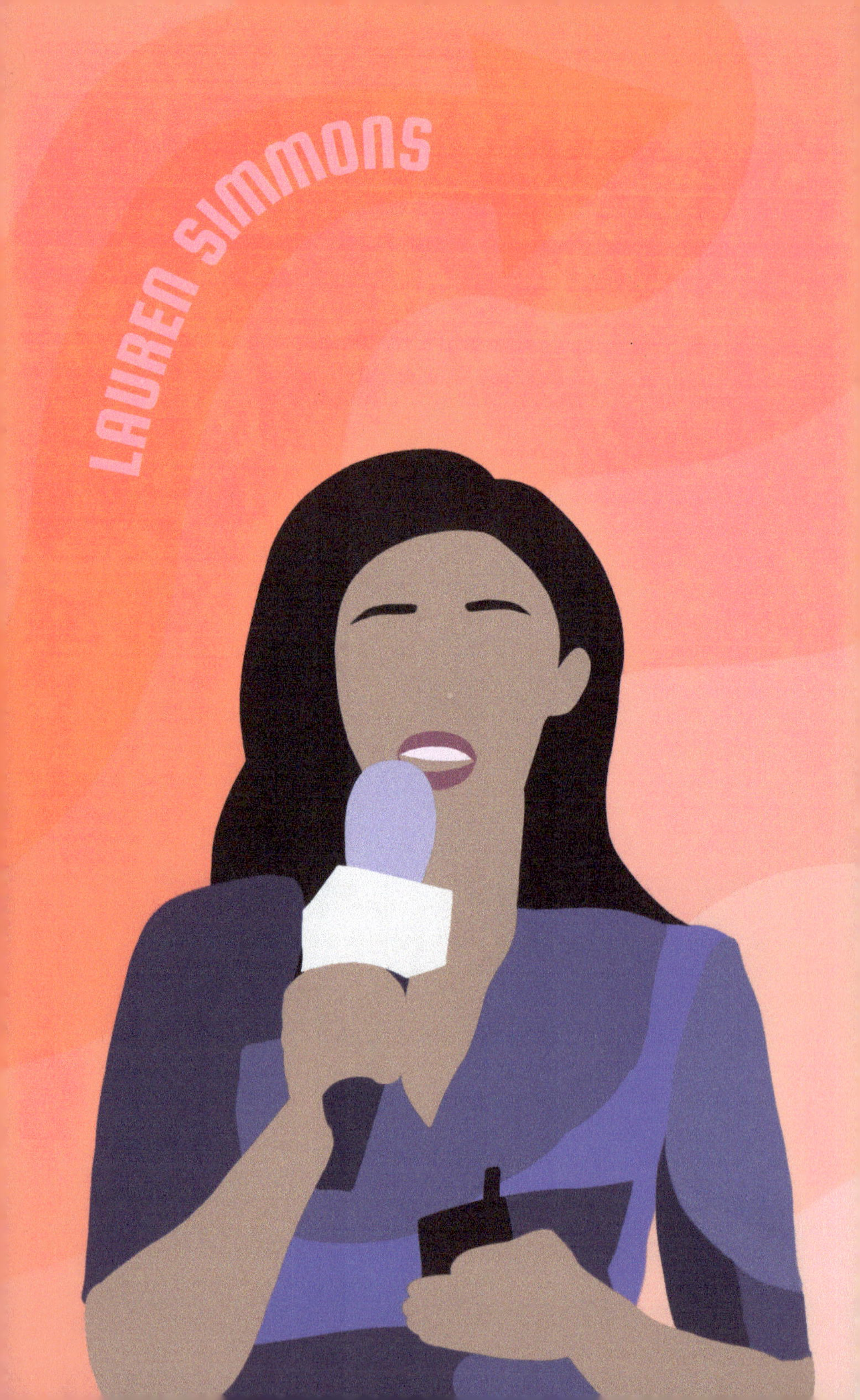
LAUREN SIMMONS

Lauren Simmons was born in 1994 to a single mother. She, along with her three siblings, grew up in Georgia. Her twin brother, who suffered from cerebral palsy, initially inspired her to pursue a career as a genetic counselor. When she graduated from Kennesaw State University in 2016, she left college with a bachelor's degree in genetics and a minor in statistics. However, when she met the CEO of Rosenblatt Securities, she was quickly taken on as an equity trader for the company. Many male coworkers doubted her abilities, some openly betting that she would fail her Series 19 exam. After passing the notoriously difficult test, her career on the trading floor began.

On March 6, 2017, at just 22 years old, Simmons claimed a position as a full-time trader on the floor of the New York Stock Exchange. She credits her success to her brother, whom she admired for his ambition and determination to succeed in spite of his disability. Lauren Simmons is now known as the youngest female trader on Wall Street, the only full-time female trader on the New York Stock Exchange, and the second African American woman to hold this position in the history of the Stock Exchange. These incredible achievements earned her the affectionate nickname, "Wolfette of Wall Street." She has also been recognized by *Ebony* Magazine, *Politico*, and various news channels. To attain these honors, Simmons has had to face both gender and race-based discrimination, as finance tends to be a male-dominated field. Despite the obstacles she has encountered, Simmons continues to encourage other young Black girls to take risks and fight for their positions in the male-dominated workforce

Ana Patricia Botín O'Shea was born in 1960 in Santander, Spain. Her father, Emilio Botín, was the Executive Chairman of Santander Bank's Spanish branch, while her mother, Paloma O'Shea, was a talented pianist. After completing her high school education at St Mary's School, Botín studied economics at Bryn Mawr College in Pennsylvania. She completed her education at Harvard Business School. Botín began her career at the investment bank JP Morgan, working there until 1988. Upon her departure from JP Morgan, Botín moved to Spain to work as a debt trader for Santander Group; she gained esteem in the company by assisting in a major acquisition valued at $495 million. By 2002, she was named Executive Chairman of Banesto, a Spanish bank. Eight years later, she was elevated to the position of the Executive Chairman of Santander UK, which is owned by Santander Bank. In 2014, she was finally appointed chair of Santander Group, making her the fourth member of the Botín family to hold this post. In addition to leading Spain's preeminent financial institution, Botín also serves as a chair of a foundation that provides financial aid to small businesses in Latin America.

Botín was first recognized as one of the top 100 most powerful women in *Forbes* Magazine in 2005. She made her return to the Magazine's coveted list in 2018, 2019, and 2020, increasing her rank to number eight. She has also been recognized for her ethical business practices and received an award for "Responsible Capitalism" in 2015. Overall, Ana Patricia Botín's renowned success can be attributed to her hard work and determination.

ANA BOTÍN

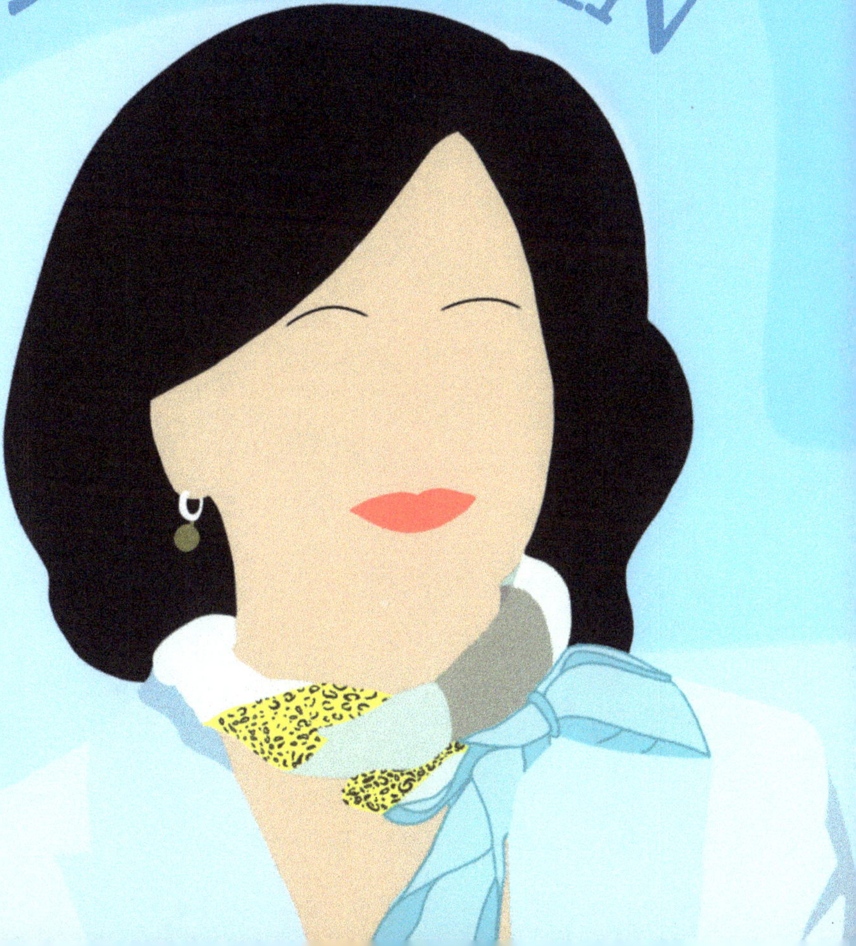

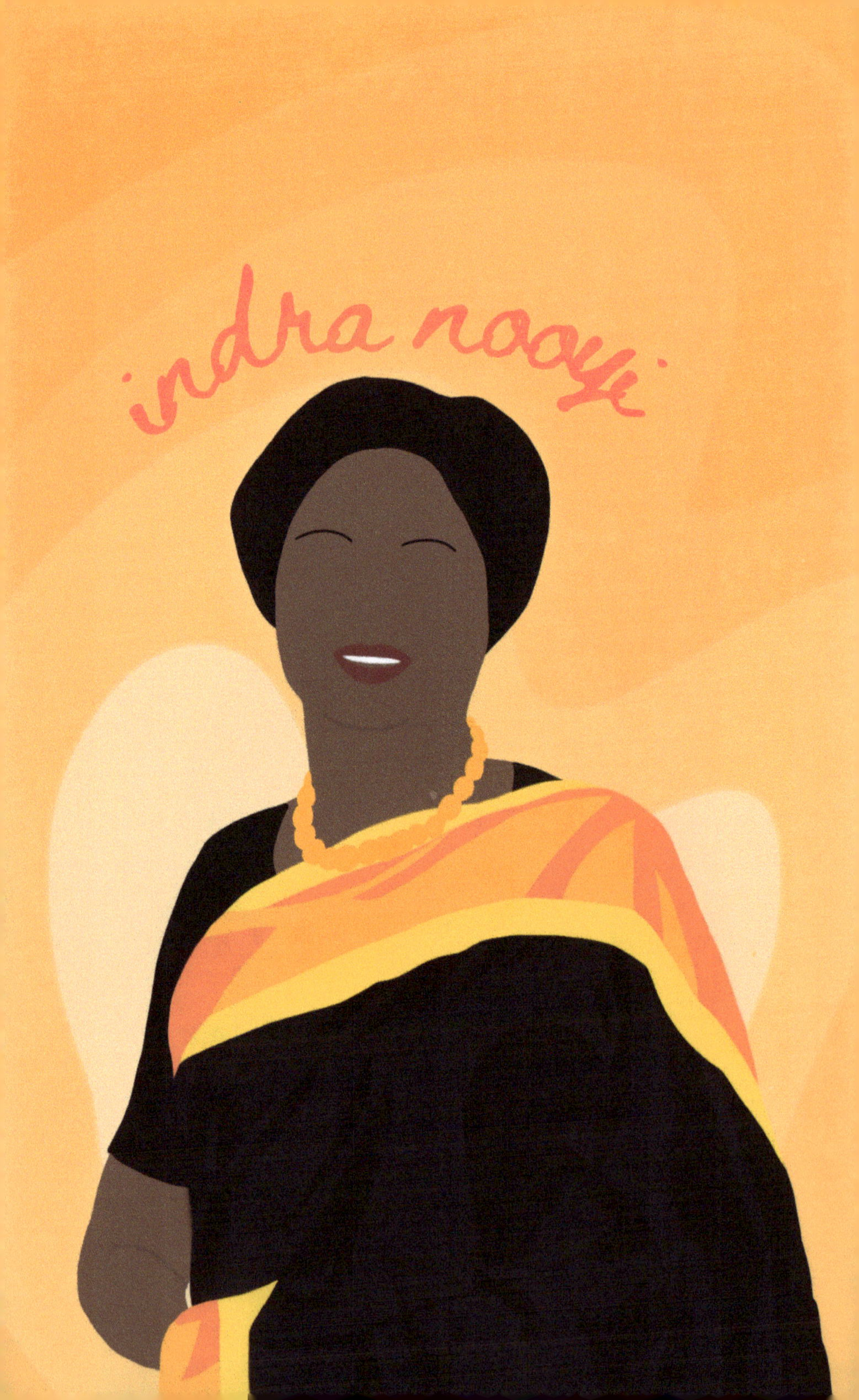
indra nooyi

Indra Nooyi was born in Chennai, India, on October 28th, 1955. After completing her secondary education at universities including Madras Christian College, the Indian Institute of Management, and Yale School of Management, Nooyi immediately joined the workforce of Boston Consulting Group. As her career progressed, Nooyi obtained increasingly influential executive positions at various companies. These experiences led to her being awarded the position of the senior vice president of corporate strategy and development at PepsiCo in 1994; just seven years later, Nooyi assumed the position of president and chief financial officer. Appointed chief executive officer (CEO) of PepsiCo in 2006, she became the first woman to hold this position in the history of the company.

Nooyi was one of just eleven female chief executive officers leading a *Fortune 500* company at the time. Furthermore, she has consistently been listed among the 100 most powerful women in the world. Her genius at business strategy and hard work earned her these honors, in spite of the discrimination-based adversity she faced as a woman in a male-dominated field. In addition to leading a company with about $64.7 billion in revenues in 2018, Nooyi was always a dedicated mother and wife. Her ability to maintain her business career while simultaneously reserving time to care for her family is widely respected.

Rosalind "Roz" Brewer was born in Detroit Michigan in 1962, the youngest of five siblings. Fascinated by math and science throughout her childhood, she planned on pursuing a career in medicine. Brewer and her siblings were the first generation of her family to earn college degrees. After completing her Bachelor's Degree in Chemistry at Spelman College, she abandoned her dream of becoming a physician to work as a research technician at Kimberly-Clark. This position granted her a path into management at this company. By 2006, Brewer was named the president of manufacturing and global operations of Kimberly-Clark. As her career continued to blossom, Brewer served as an executive-level manager at Walmart, Sam's Club, and Starbucks.

Throughout her career, Brewer has made history several times. She was the first female Chief Operating Officer of Starbucks; as a Black woman, she recognized the need to counter racial bias within the company. One of her tweets calling for more diversity in her workplace resulted in hate messages and death threats, which fueled her determination to bring about change. She has also implemented policies to improve the sustainability of companies under her leadership. Furthermore, Brewer was the first-ever woman to sit on the Amazon board. She was also recognized as the third Black woman to lead a Fortune 500 Company and was listed among the most powerful women in *Forbes* Magazine. With such an accomplished and groundbreaking career, Brewer has been recognized as a role model for young Black girls while continually advocating for sustainability and equality in the world of business.

ROSALIND BREWER

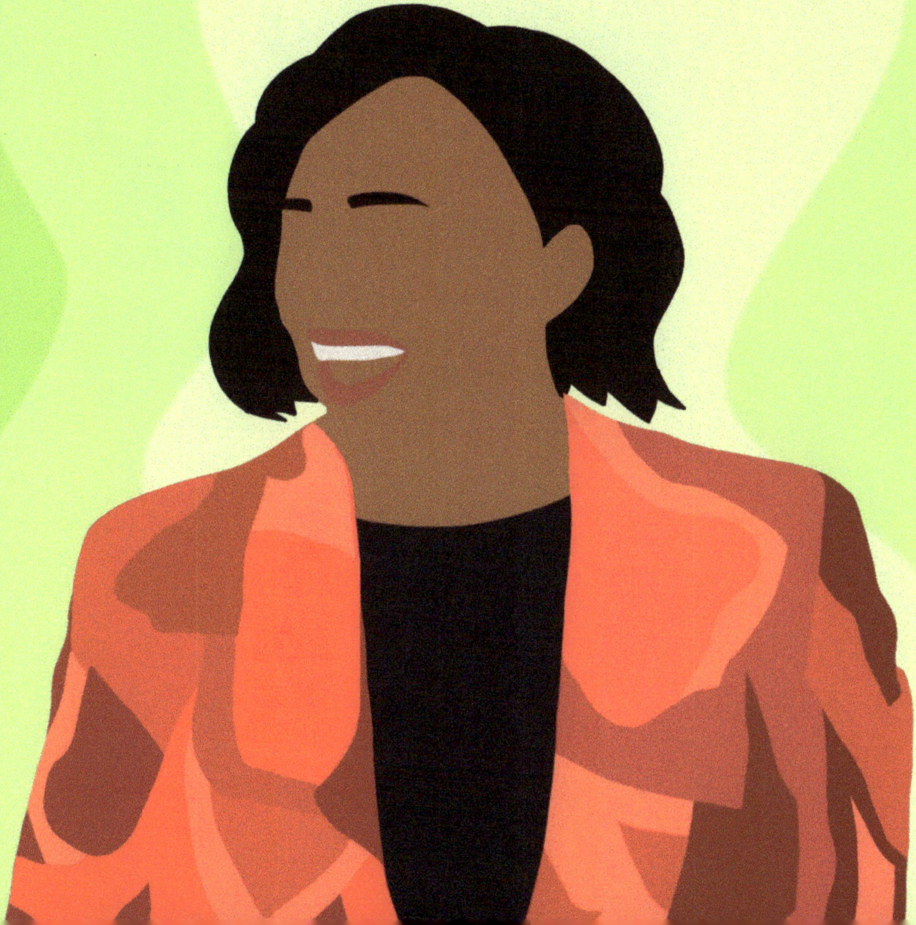

PART 2:

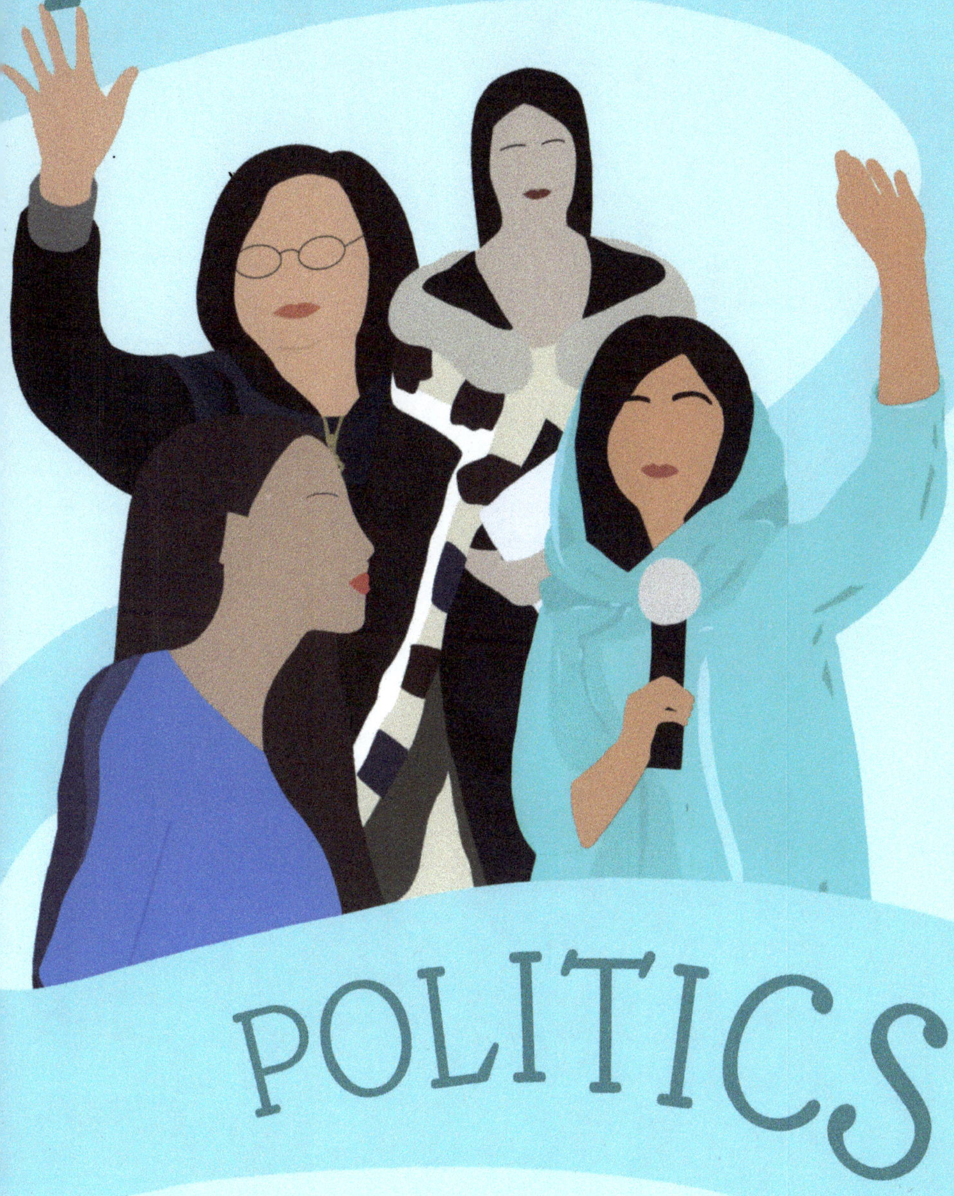

POLITICS

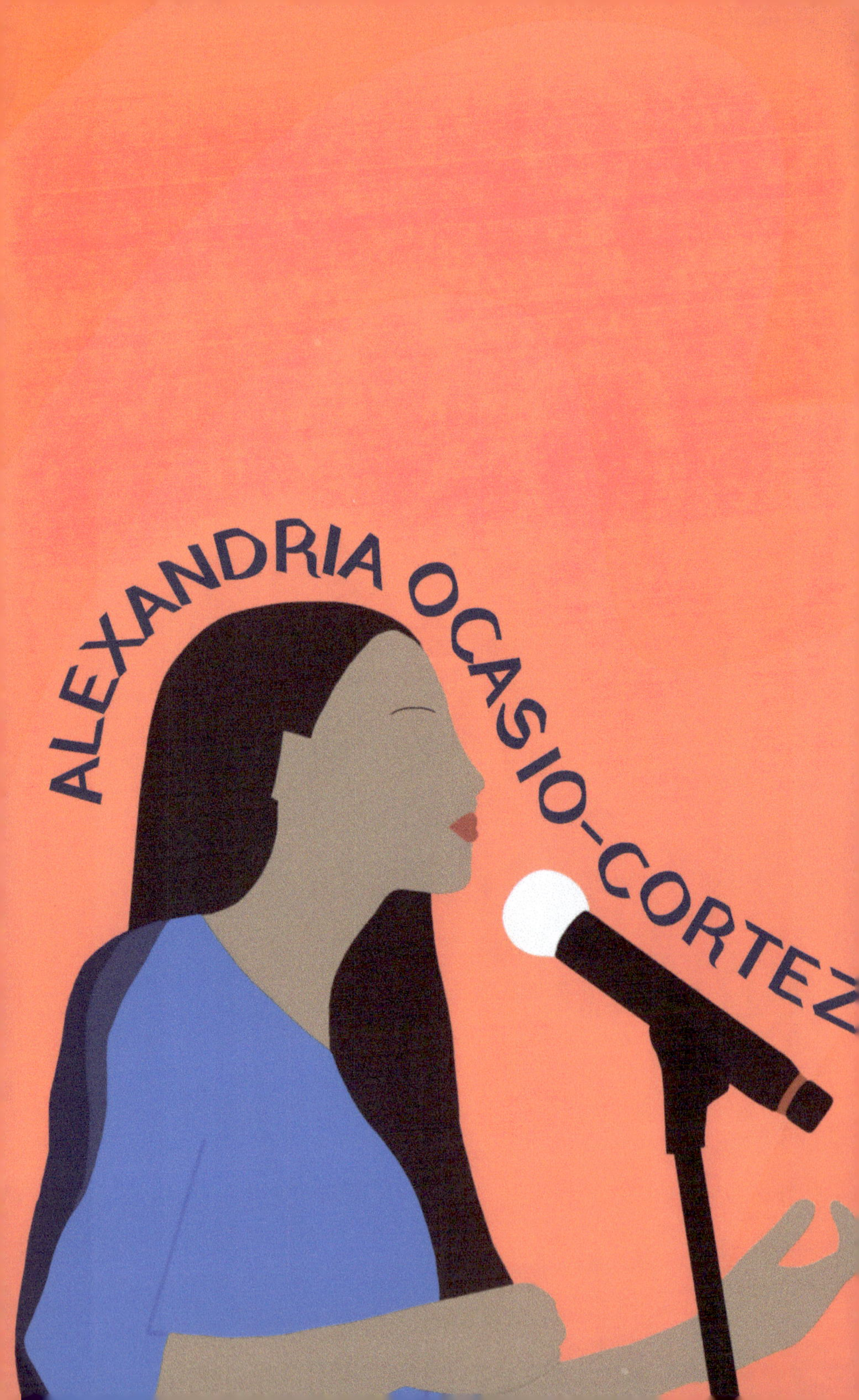
ALEXANDRIA OCASIO-CORTEZ

Alexandria Ocasio-Cortez (AOC), born to a Puerto Rican family in New York City on October 13, 1989, experienced income inequality and social injustice throughout her childhood. Her working-class family struggled to support themselves during the Great Recession. Diagnosed with lung cancer when AOC was just a teenager, her father passed away in 2008, forcing Ocasio-Cortez and her mother to work multiple low-wage jobs as they were threatened with foreclosure. She attended Boston University, majoring in Economics and International Relations, while maintaining an internship at Senator Ted Kennedy's office. As a mere teenager and the only Spanish-speaker, Ocasio-Cortez assumed the responsibility of helping distressed immigrant families, separated by ICE, navigate the system.

Ocasio-Cortez continued her journey as an activist directly after her graduation, serving as the Educational Director of the National Hispanic Institute non-profit while simultaneously supporting herself through bartending and waitressing. She worked as a volunteer organizer for Bernie Sanders during the 2016 election, gaining the political skills and experience to begin her own campaign for Congress in New York's 14th Congressional District. AOC proclaimed in her viral advertisement, "Women like me aren't supposed to run for office." She won her position in Congress following a revolutionary victory against 10-term Congressman Joe Crowley in the state's Democratic Primary; elected at just 28 years old, AOC is now the youngest woman ever to be elected to Congress. Her unwavering resolve to serve working-class people and advocate for social and environmental justice characterizes her political career.

Tsai Ing-Wen, born in 1956, was the youngest of eleven siblings in her family. Ing-Wen's childhood involvement in her parents' auto shop instilled in her the value of hard work and resilience. After graduating from the College of Law of National Taiwan University, she went on to earn degrees from Cornell University Law School and the University of London. Ing-Wen then moved back to Taiwan to work as a law professor. With her excellent education, she obtained a position as the Chief Legal Advisor to the Fair Trade Commission. In 2000, Ing-Wen saw the start of her political career, as she was appointed chair of the Mainland Affairs Council. She also worked in the National Security Council before being elected the legislator-at-large for the Democratic Progressive Party (DPP) of Taiwan. After rising through the ranks of the political party, she eventually won the election for the DPP chair; this election would name her the first female to serve as a chair in a Taiwanese political party. She would also become Taiwan's first female presidential candidate, winning election as the nation's 14th president. As a member of a family with no political connections, Ing-Wen, nevertheless, became the first female head of state in Asia who was not born into that role. In 2020, Ing-Wen was re-elected as the 15th president of Taiwan.

Throughout her political career, Ing-Wen has advocated for the rights of underrepresented groups. She pushed the legalization of same-sex marriage in Taiwan, making history as it became the first Asian country to do so. Knowing the struggles of the working class in Taiwan, she has also endorsed pension reform policies and labor laws. Raising the nation's minimum wage in her first term in the presidential office became another success for Ing-Wen. Her tireless efforts to break boundaries and advocate for her people captivated the citizens of Taiwan, as well as people around the world.

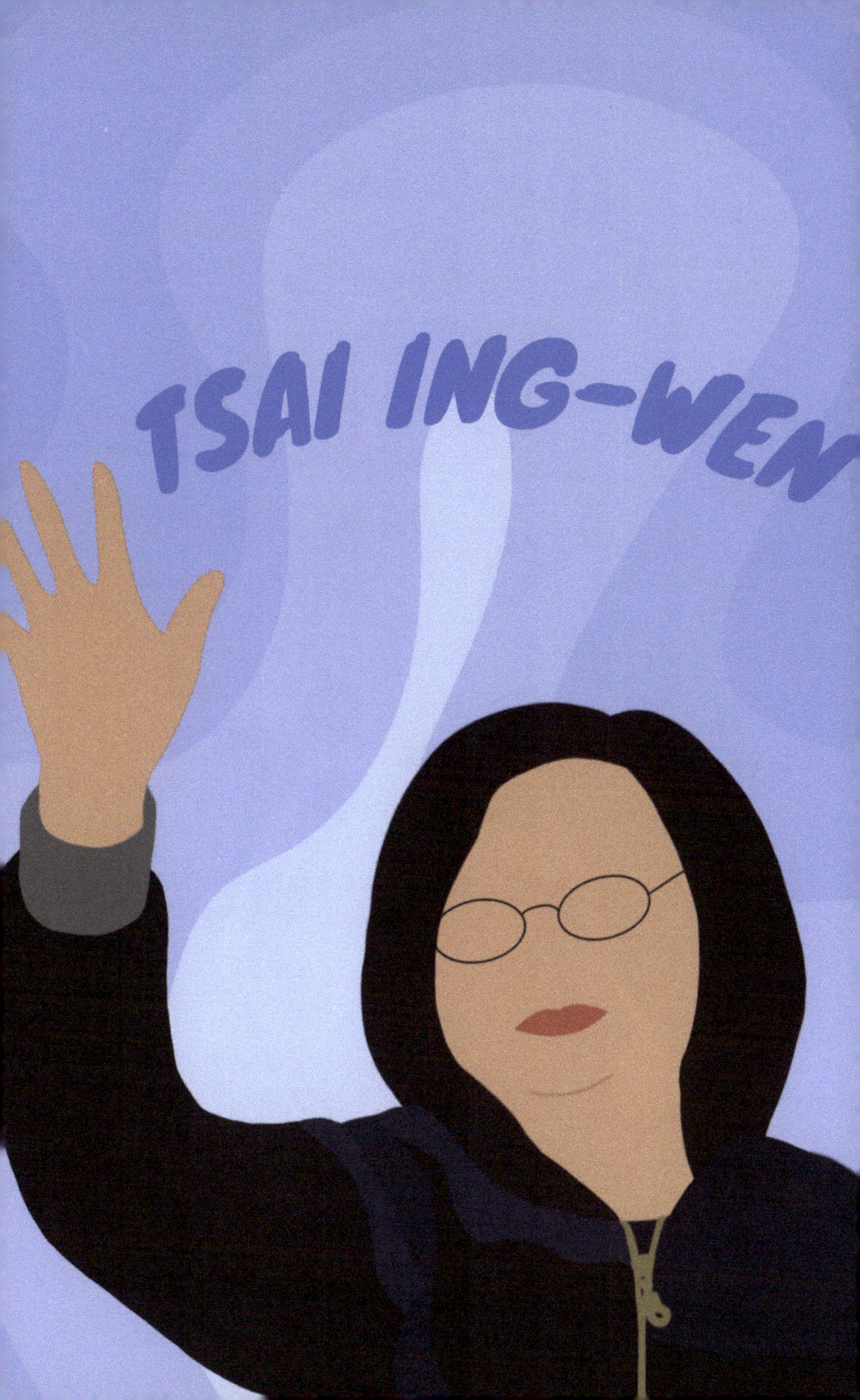
TSAI ING-WEN

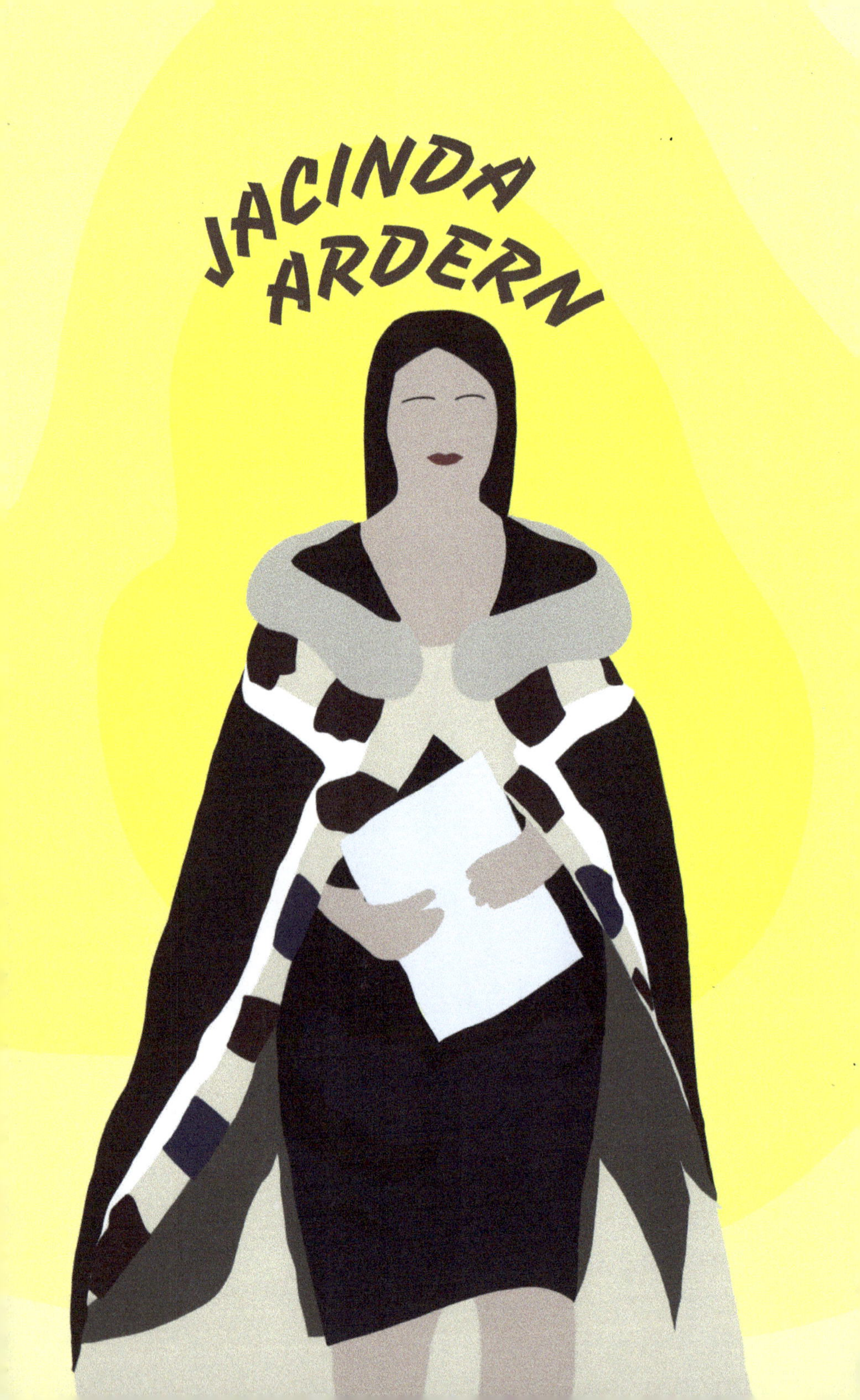
JACINDA
ARDERN

Jacinda Ardern was born in Hamilton, New Zealand, in 1980. Spending the first years of her life in an area with rampant gang activity, Ardern was exposed to poverty and starvation. After relocating to Morrinsville, Ardern continued her schooling and went on to attend the University of Waikato. There, she earned a bachelor's degree in Communication Studies. Her awareness of the struggles of the impoverished would inspire her career in politics.

At just 17 years old, Ardern became an active member of the Labor Party. After assisting in the reelection campaign of Harry Duynehoven, Ardern began work as a researcher for Phil Goff. She then moved on to work with Prime Minister Helen Clark, who had been her personal hero and inspiration; at this time, Clark was the second woman to ever hold the position of Prime Minister in New Zealand. Following this stint, Ardern spent two and a half years in the cabinet office of Tony Blair, Britain's Prime Minister at the time. By 2008, Ardern was chosen to be the Labor Party's candidate, representing the Waikato district in Parliament. Although she lost this election, she went on to enter the House of Representatives where she pursued her goals of increasing the inclusivity of New Zealand natives in the education system and responding to climate change.

In the 2017 election for Prime Minister, Ardern sought to oust Bill English of the National Party from his position and planned to implement free secondary education, decriminalize abortion, and improve the living conditions of impoverished and marginalized populations. She garnered support from young voters and women, who saw potential in her ideas. As her public presence increased, she advocated for fairer treatment of women in the workplace. She soon won the role of New Zealand's 40th Prime Minister in a landslide election. In this position, she became the youngest woman to head a government in modern history. Ardern is also one of just a few female prime ministers currently in office. Indeed, her powerful advocacy for a multitude of social causes has set Jacinda Ardern apart from the rest.

Malala Yousafzai was born on July 12, 1997, in Mingora, Pakistan. Despite the custom of preferring a male child over a female in her culture, Malala's father, Ziauddin Yousafzai, was intent on raising her with the same respect and opportunity that a boy would receive. Ziauddin was a feminist and educational activist who instilled these values in his daughter at a young age. Malala's father was known for founding a school in Swat Valley, Pakistan, in which girls and boys could learn together. In 2008, the school was forced to close as the terrorist group the Taliban imposed a ban on the education of girls, despite the peaceful protest efforts of Malala's father.

Malala, greatly valuing her education, felt obligated to protest this ban through public speeches and activism. Unfortunately, her valiant efforts made her a target of the Taliban, who attacked her on October 9th, 2012. At just 15 years of age, Malala was shot in the head on the bus ride on her way home from school. Treated in a hospital in Birmingham, England, Malala underwent two surgeries and weeks of recovery. By the end of her recuperation, she was able to join her family in their new Birmingham home where she found that her dramatic story gained worldwide interest.

Despite the traumatic events she had experienced, Malala's passion for activism only strengthened with time. She founded the Malala Fund in 2013 and continued to advocate for women's rights to education around the world. To date, her organization has raised about 22 million dollars which it has invested in establishing educational equality. In 2014, Malala was awarded the Nobel Peace Prize, making her the youngest-ever Nobel laureate.

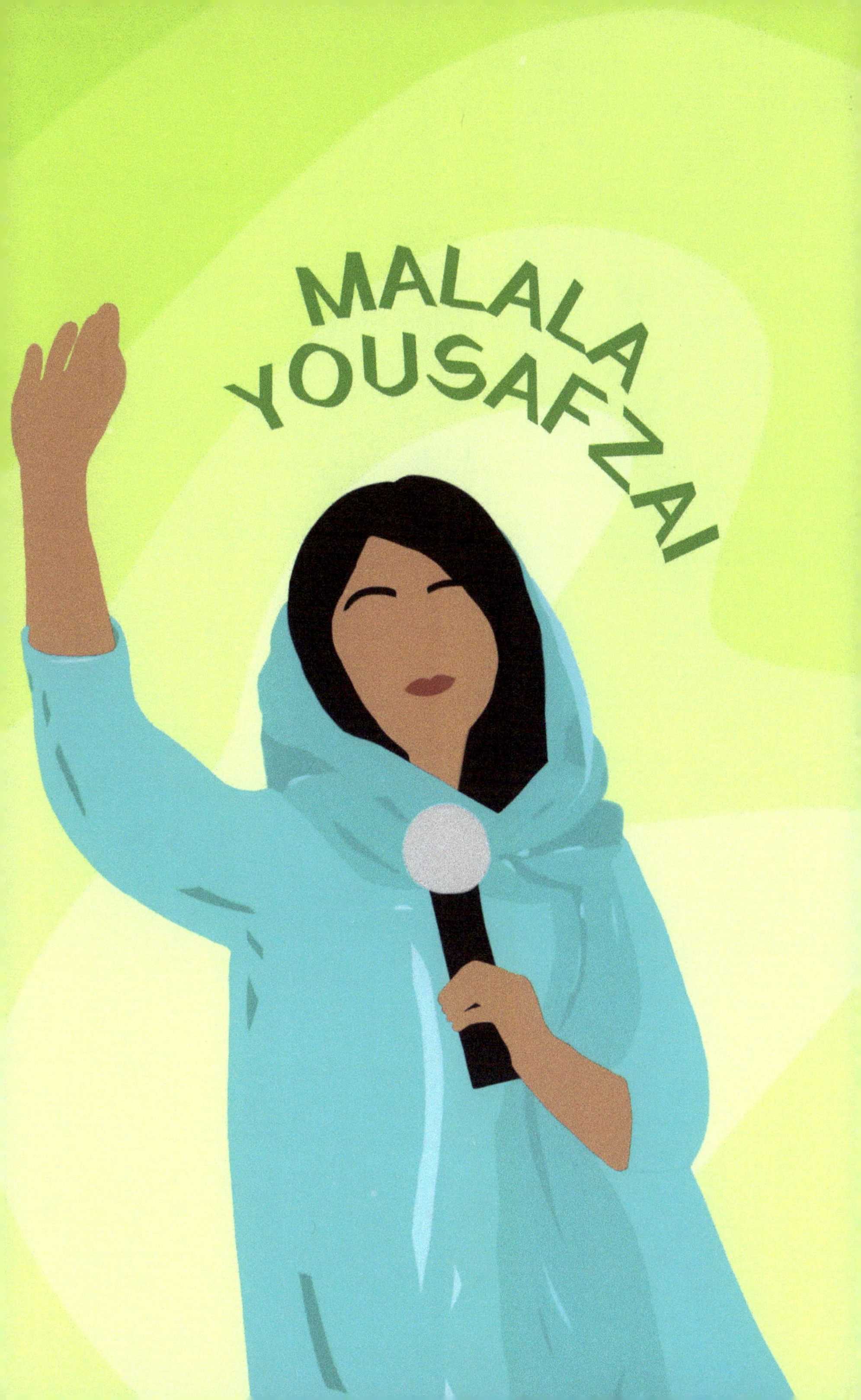
MALALA
YOUSAFZAI

PART 3:

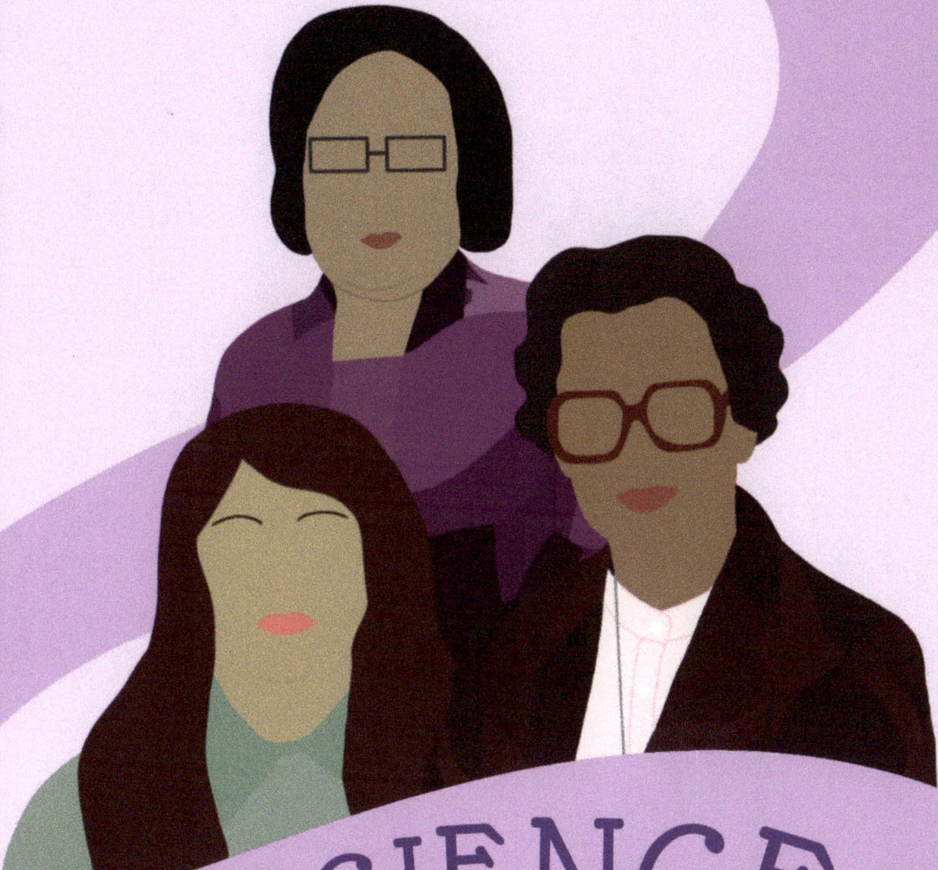

THE SCIENCES

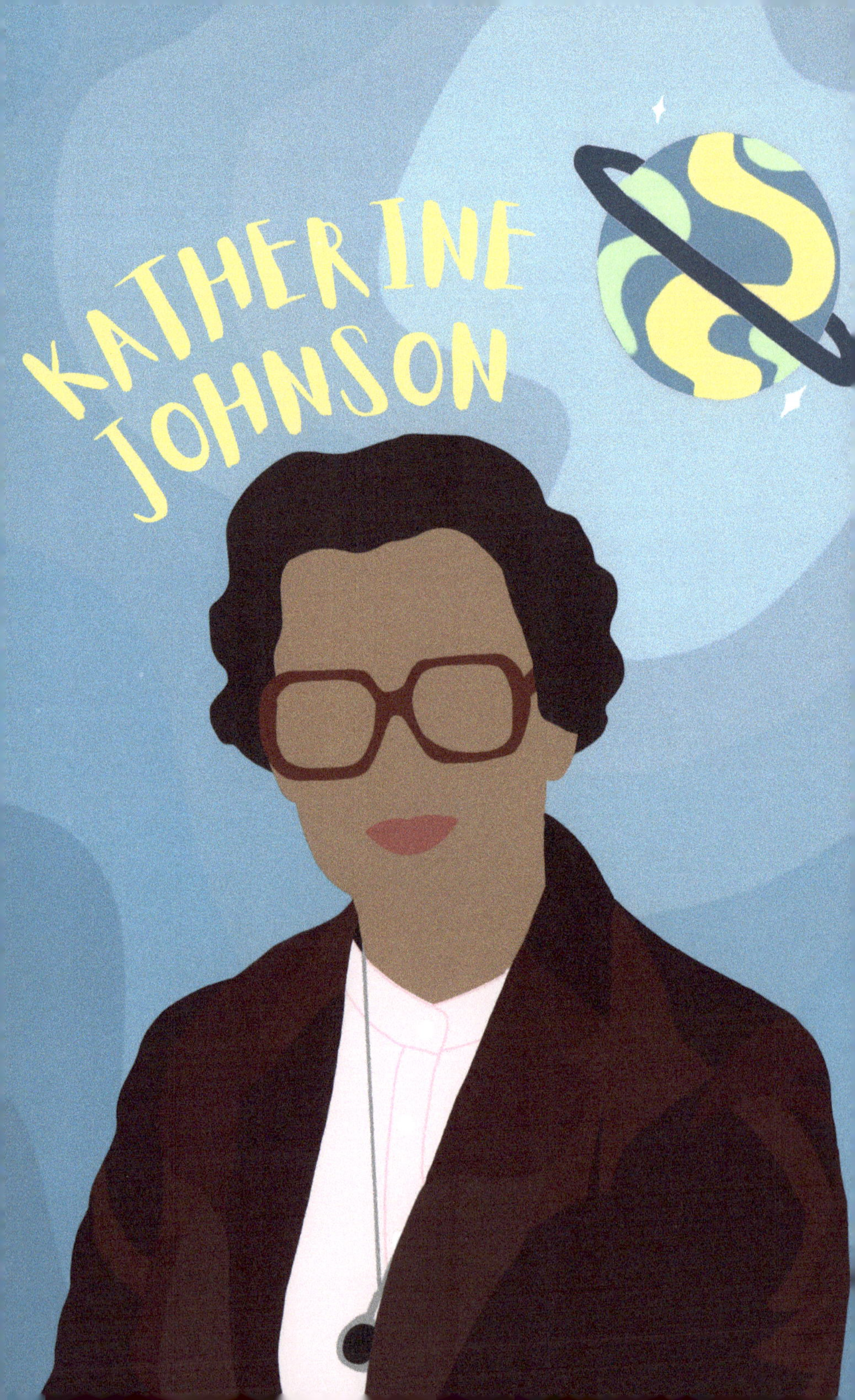
KATHERINE
JOHNSON

Katherine Johnson was born in 1918 in West Virginia. Despite an early display of talent in mathematics, she was unable to attend school in her home county as it did not allow African Americans access to public education past eighth grade. Her parents, determined to find her an education suited to her ability, enrolled her in a nearby county. Starting high school at just 10 years of age, Johnson graduated at 14 and attended West Virginia State College. The young genius took advantage of the opportunities her college offered her, enrolling in every mathematics course available and securing mentorship from professors. After graduating with degrees in mathematics and French, she started teaching at a school that offered education to Black students. She went on to attend graduate school as one of just three Black students and the only woman in the program.

Johnson's dream of becoming a research mathematician proved difficult because of race and gender-based discrimination in the field. She finally found a job with the National Advisory Committee for Aeronautics. Its Langley Memorial Aeronautical Laboratory was open to hiring African Americans, so Johnson began her work there in 1953. For her first five years at the laboratory, she functioned as a computer, performing mathematical calculations by hand in a segregated office. For another eight years, Johnson worked in the Spacecraft Controls Branch as an aerospace technologist. Her work was crucial to the 1961 space flight in which Alan Shepard became the first American to enter space. She would also perform calculations for Project Mercury, Apollo 11, Apollo 13, the Space Shuttle program and the Earth Resources Satellite. When NASA first introduced electronic computers, they called upon Johnson to confirm their accuracy. The legendary "computer" earned a name for herself in the field of aeronautics, despite the segregation and discrimination she experienced along the way. Her genius and hard work forced supervisors to overlook the fact that she was consigned to working in the "Colored Computers" office as one of the only women in her division. Katherine Johnson is truly an unsung American hero!

Radia Joy Perlman was born on December 18, 1951 in Portsmouth, Virginia. She grew up in New Jersey where both of her parents worked as engineers for the US government. Radia was an incredibly gifted child who excelled in her academic career, taking a particular interest in math and science. She enrolled in her first programming class in high school, with no expectation of success. Perlman received both her undergraduate and master's degrees in mathematics at the Massachusetts Institute of Technology (MIT), all while working as a part-time programmer at the MIT Artificial Intelligence Laboratory. At MIT, Perlman noticed a glaring gender disparity, with about 50 women in a class of 1,000 students. The university had dedicated only a single dorm for females, validating its intention to admit a scant number of women.

Joining the Digital Equipment Corporation (DEC) in 1980, Radia immediately made an impression on her supervisors. At the time, the company was faced with issues in sharing files between computers. To solve this problem, she developed the revolutionary spanning-tree protocol. This invention earned her the title of "Mother of the Internet." In the span of her career, Perlman has obtained over 80 patents and 10 awards for her work, including the title of 2004 Inventor of the Year. In addition to her notable engineering career, Perlman also became an affiliate professor at University of Washington while also lecturing at universities such as Harvard and MIT.

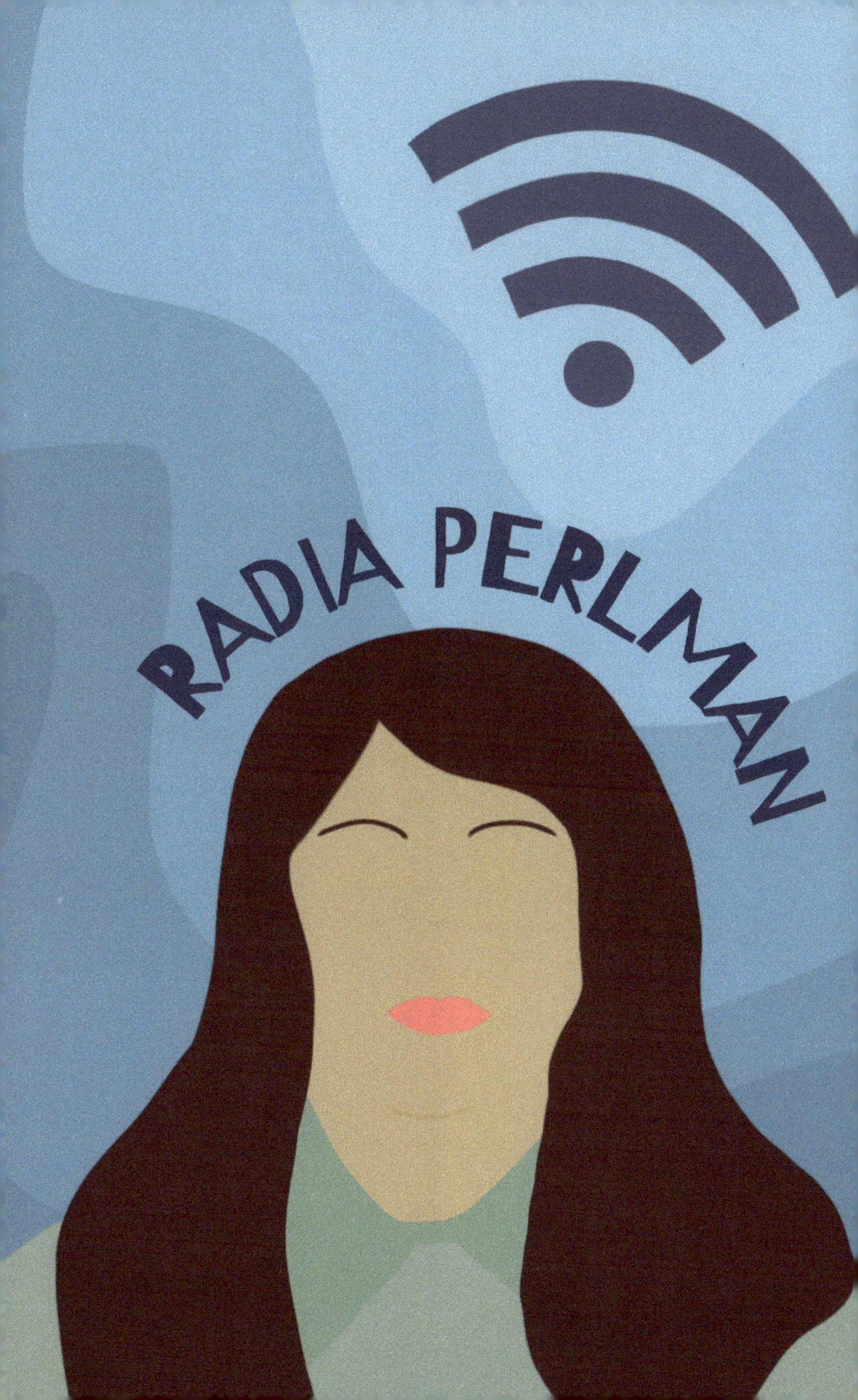
RADIA PERLMAN

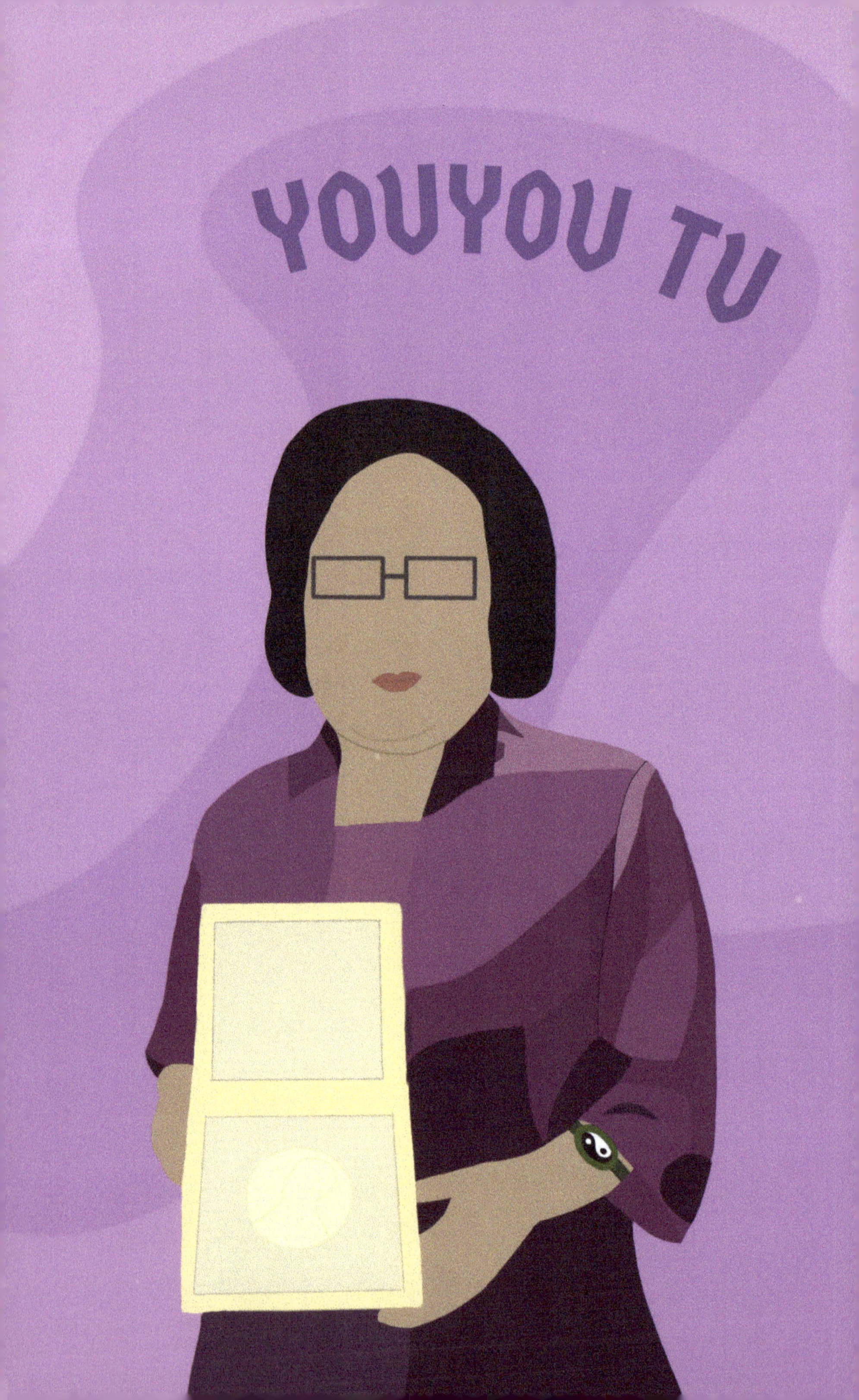
YOUYOU TU

Tu Youou was born in Ningbo, Zhejiang, China on December 30, 1930. In naming her "Youyou," her father was inspired by an ancient Chinese line of poetry about the plant that, coincidentally, would serve as the basis for her most groundbreaking work. A tuberculosis infection at the age of 15, which forced her to take a break from her high school education, motivated Tu's interest in medical research. After attending college and medical school from 1951 to 1955, she obtained a degree in pharmacology and began her career at the Academy of Traditional Chinese Medicine in Beijing.

During the Vietnam War in 1967, Tu was tasked with leading a team of scientists in finding a treatment for malaria in a covert government project. Researching existing Chinese folk remedies, her team tested the efficacy of 380 different extracts in curing malaria. Tu found that the sweet wormwood plant (qinghao), *Artemisia annua,* was effective in treating the disease in both mice and monkeys. After a year of clinical trials and experimentation, Tu's team finally extracted the active component of the medicine and named it *qinghaosu.* Their research findings were disseminated to global populations in the 1980's. This revolutionary discovery saved millions of lives and, accordingly, earned Youyou Tu the Nobel Prize for Physiology in Medicine in 2015. She is now employed at the Academy of Traditional Chinese Medical Sciences as their Chief Scientist.

In addition to her work in the field of pharmacology, Tu has also been praised for her dedication to her family throughout her career. While excelling in her demanding profession, she was also responsible for caring for her two daughters. Her husband was sent away by the government, prompting Tu to essentially raise her children as a single parent, with the assistance of her parents and a Beijing daycare center. Despite these personal challenges, Tu was still able to make a significant impact through her career in STEM.

PART 4:

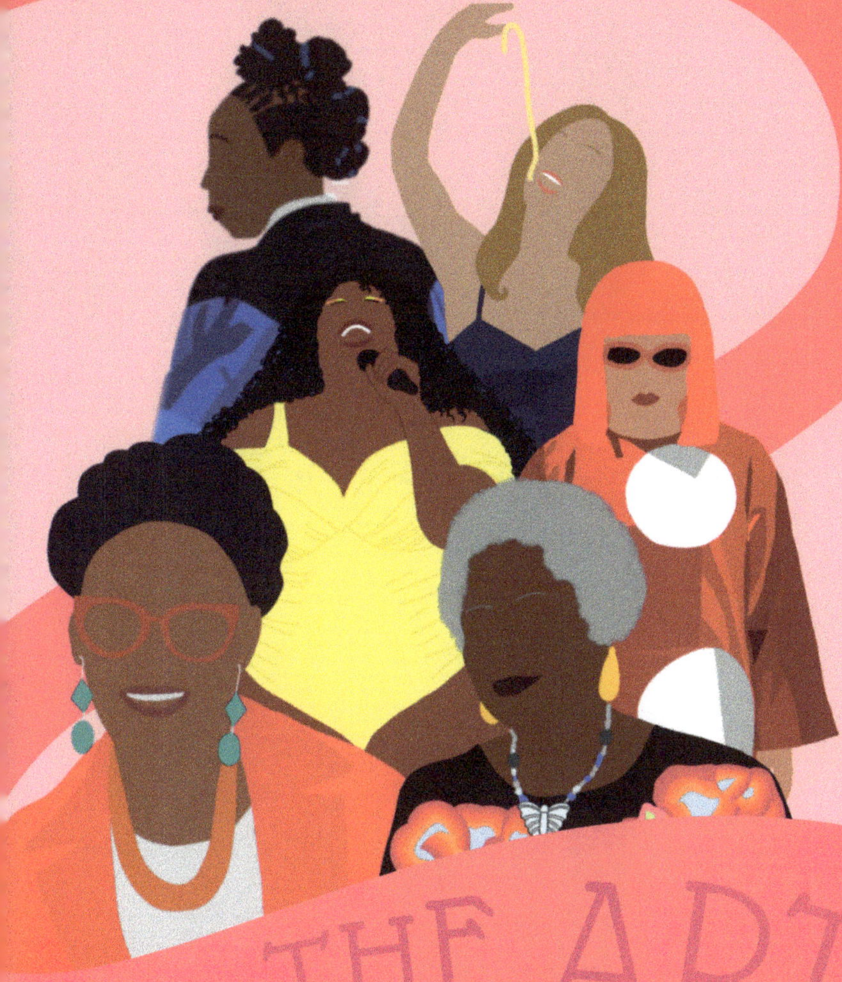

THE ARTS

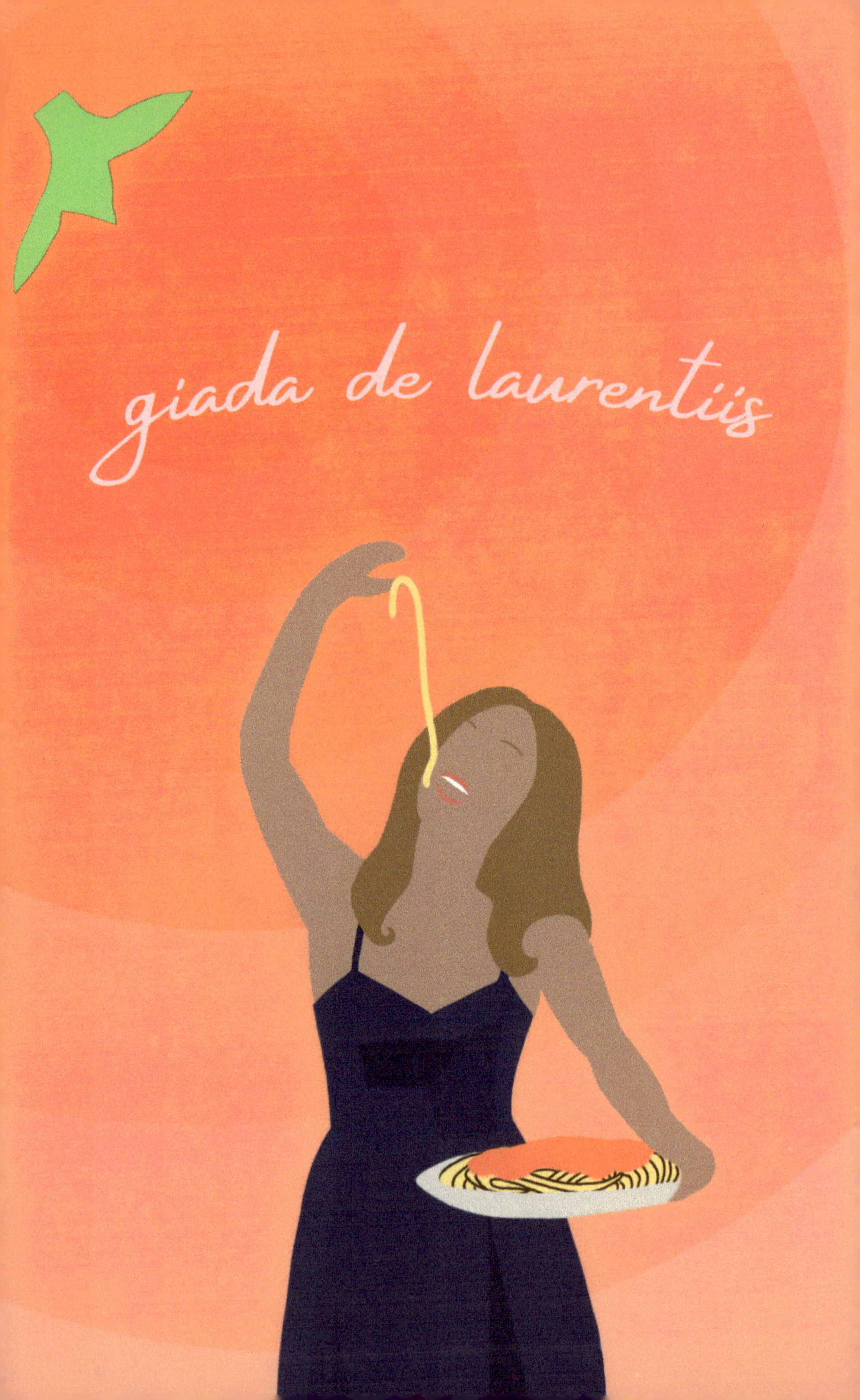
giada de laurentiis

Giada Pamela De Benedetti was born in 1970 to a family of actors and film producers. Her interest, however, was in the culinary arts. Throughout her childhood, Giada experimented in her family's kitchen and in her grandfather's restaurant. Following her parent's divorce, Giada moved to Southern California and adopted her mother's last name. Here, she attended school and university before moving to Paris for professional training at the esteemed culinary school Le Cordon Bleu. After completing her training, Giada worked in Los Angeles restaurants and later founded her own catering business, GDL Foods. In 2002, she was contacted by the Food Network, which premiered her cooking show just a year later. This show was the first of many that Giada hosted and appeared in throughout her career. In 2014, she opened her own restaurant, GIADA, in Las Vegas, Nevada. She has also shared her personal recipes and cooking advice in several best-selling cookbooks.

Giada is known as an inspirational chef as she often speaks about her passion for cooking and the way it has helped heal her relationship with food. After experiencing health issues caused by her imbalanced diet, she embarked on her journey to a happier, healthier way to live. One of her cookbooks details recipes that she used to achieve wellness while still enjoying what she ate. Giada continues to be an inspiration for those who harbor a love of cooking.

Lena Waithe, born in 1984 in Chicago, Illinois, had her career path decided by the age of seven. She loved television writing, a passion which her single mother and grandmother firmly supported. After attending school in Chicago, she earned a degree in cinema and television arts at Columbia College. Completing her senior year of college in Los Angeles, she remained there to establish her career, which began with the role of production assistant for directors Gina Prince-Bythewood and Mara Brock Akil. These roles led to her landing acting roles in programs with Lisa Kudrow and Aziz Ansari. Her upbringing in Chicago inspired Waithe to create and produce "The Chi," a show that provides a unique perspective on life in the Southside of Chicago. Waithe created the show to portray the beauty and complexity of her hometown, rather than merely the violence and gang-activity with which it is often associated.

Throughout Waithe's career, she has expressed her desire to allow more Black and LGBTQ+ representation in television and film. Being a Black queer woman, Waithe recognizes the lack of diversity in the screen writing industry; with her position as Co-Chair of the Committee of Black Writers, she aims to provide more Black women and men access to screen writing positions. Additionally, she has often incorporated queer and Black representation into her programs. In fact, an episode she wrote in the show, "Master of None" discusses one aspect of the queer coming-out experience, inspired by her personal life. This episode earned Waithe the GLAAD Media Award for Outstanding Individual Episode at the 29th Annual GLAAD Media Awards. Waithe also voiced the first openly queer character in the Disney franchise in the film *Onward*. Some of her films also feature politically-charged content, presented through comedy, which garners attention to social issues under the guise of entertainment. With all of Waithe's work for the many communities she supports, she has become a powerful inspiration to activists and members of the film industry, alike.

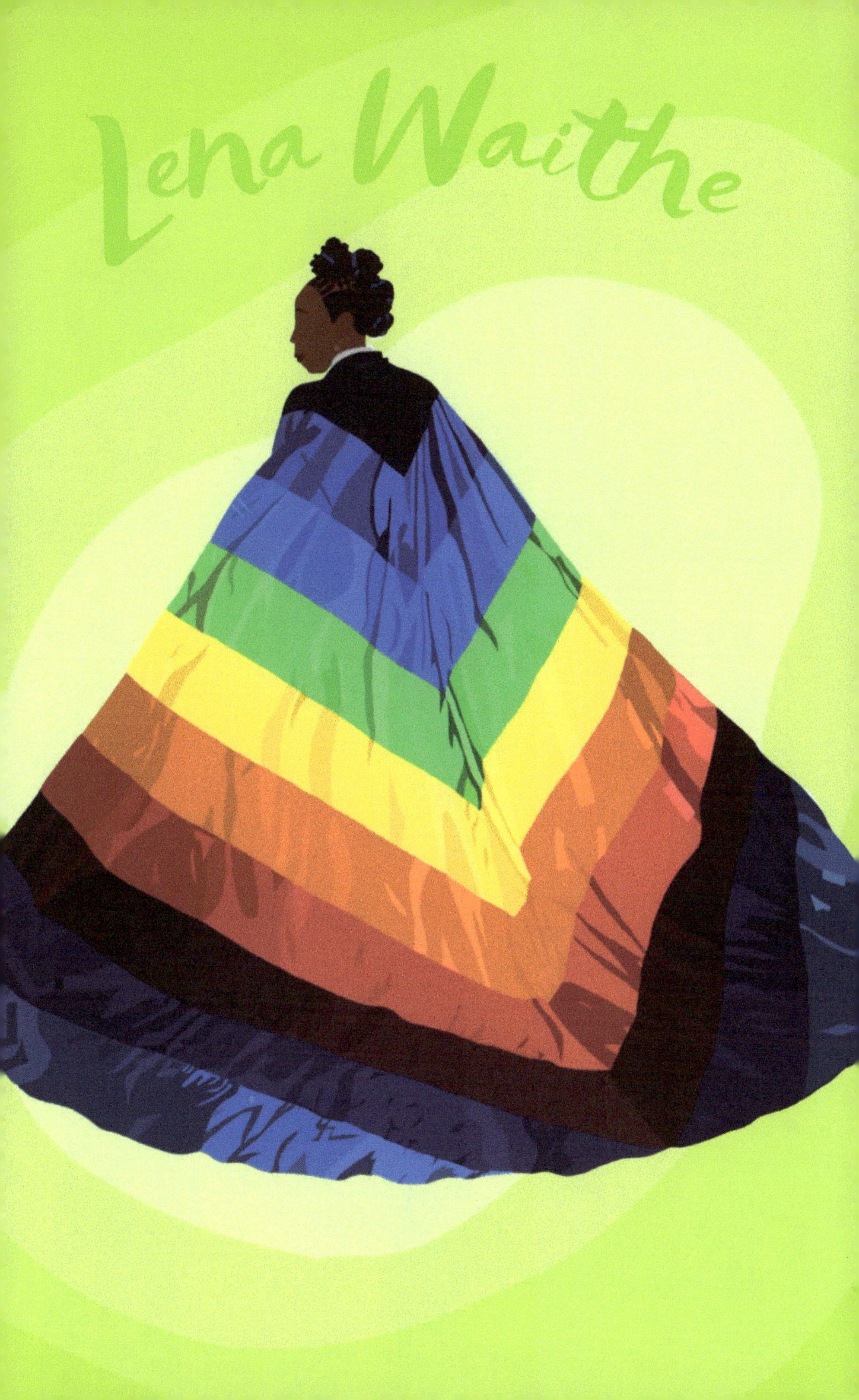
Lena Waithe

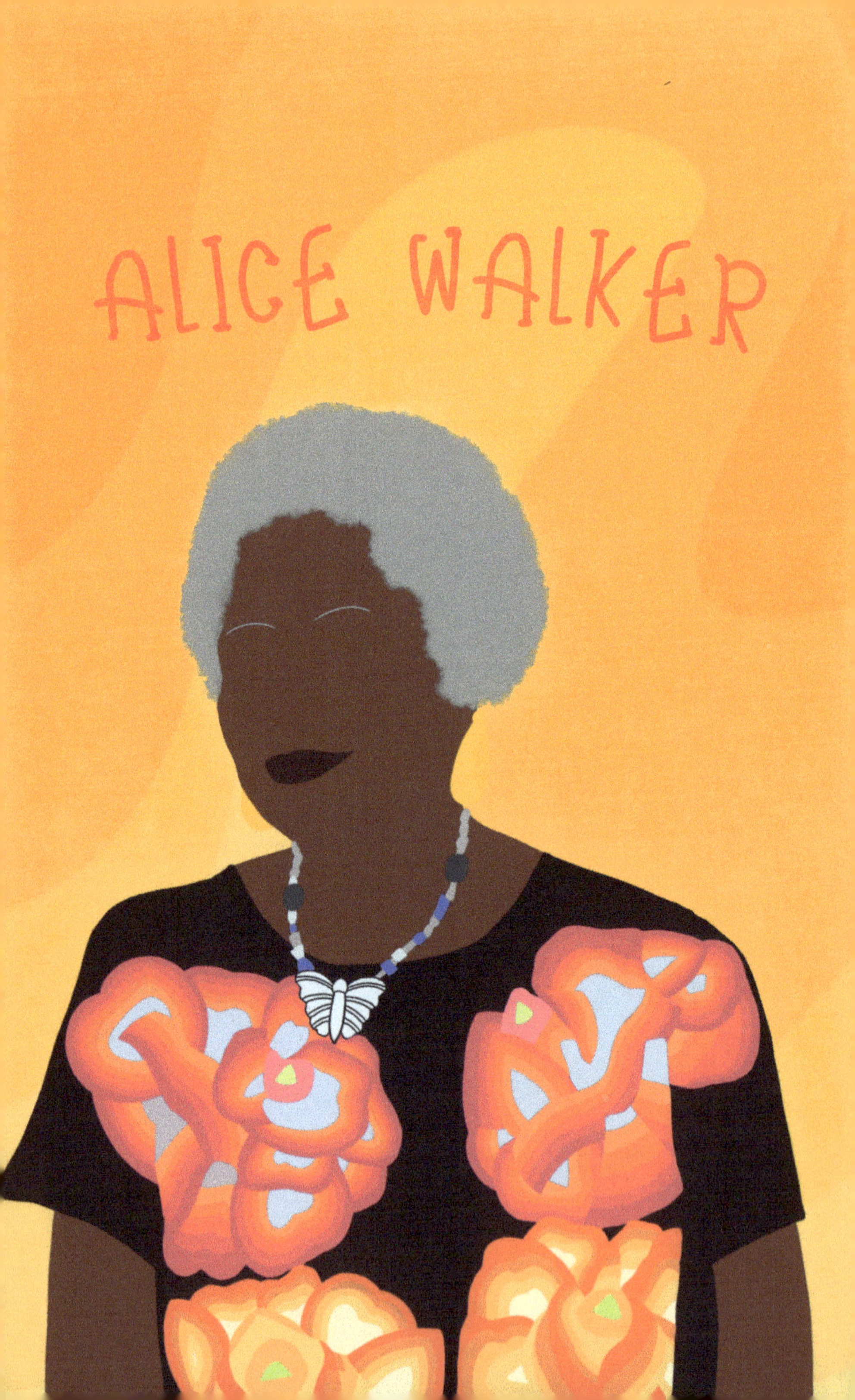
ALICE WALKER

Alice Malsenoir Tallulah-Kate Walker was born on February 9th, 1944, to Minnie Tallulah Grant and Willie Lee Walker. Partially blinded in an accident at 8 years of age, Walker took to writing as a pastime, finding a lifelong passion. As a shy and reclusive child, Alice had been teased for the scar tissue that grew over her injured eye; however, reading and writing poetry became her emotional outlet. In 1961, she enrolled at Spelman College, a historically Black liberal arts college, where she was awarded a scholarship. After her graduation, she became involved in the ongoing civil rights movement and taught, at the University of Massachusetts Boston, the first course on African American female writers offered in the United States. Also involved in the feminism movement, primarily led by middle-class White women, Walker pioneered a movement known as "womanism," which emphasized the racist, classist, and sexist oppression of African American women, specifically.

In another milestone, Walker married Melvyn Rosenman Leventhal in the first legal interracial marriage in the heavily segregated state of Mississippi. This short-lived marriage ended in divorce in 1976. Thereafter, Walker began publishing her literary work, including short stories and essays, in addition to teaching. Her revolutionary debut novel, *The Third Life of Grange Copeland,* detailed the reality of life as a Black man in the early twentieth century. Her various award-winning novels, short stories, and poems exposed her audience to African American culture, highlighting the struggles of this community. Walker also covered sensitive and controversial topics such as abortion and suicical ideation in her work. Her most famous novel, *The Color Purple,* earned the National Book Award for Fiction (Hardcover) in 1983. In the same year, Walker was awarded the Pulitzer Prize for Fiction for this book, becoming the first Black woman to earn this honor. Her sensational story was adapted into a motion picture just three years following its release. She went on to win two Lillian Smith Book Awards in 1973 and 1984 for *Revolutionary Petunias and Other Poems* and *In Search of Our Mothers' Gardens: Womanist Prose.*

Glenis Redmond was born on August 27, 1963 to a family of Air Force members. Because she traveled throughout her childhood, Redmond considers herself a "native of nowhere." Her creative and artistic personality became apparent as she took up reading and dance in her early childhood. Redmond's interest in poetry first bloomed during her stay in Italy. Years later-- when she had settled in Richmond, Virginia, pregnant with twins and in school to obtain a PhD in psychology-- she reunited with her passion for poetry. She then left her program to pursue her true calling as a poet.

Redmond's beautiful poetry pays tribute to her roots as a Black woman. Following a devastating cancer diagnosis, she also used poetry as an emotional outlet and a solace during a difficult period of her life. Redmond's unique prose and passionate voice earned her recognition at myriad festivals and award competitions. Not only does she share her personal story through her work, but she also inspires others to do the same, as a teaching poet. By touring the world and sharing her gift through workshops, Redmond continues to encourage children and adults alike to find their poetic voice. In doing this, she has partnered with nonprofit organizations, homeless shelters, and half-way homes to inspire others to find peace and healing in poetry.

GLENIS REDMOND

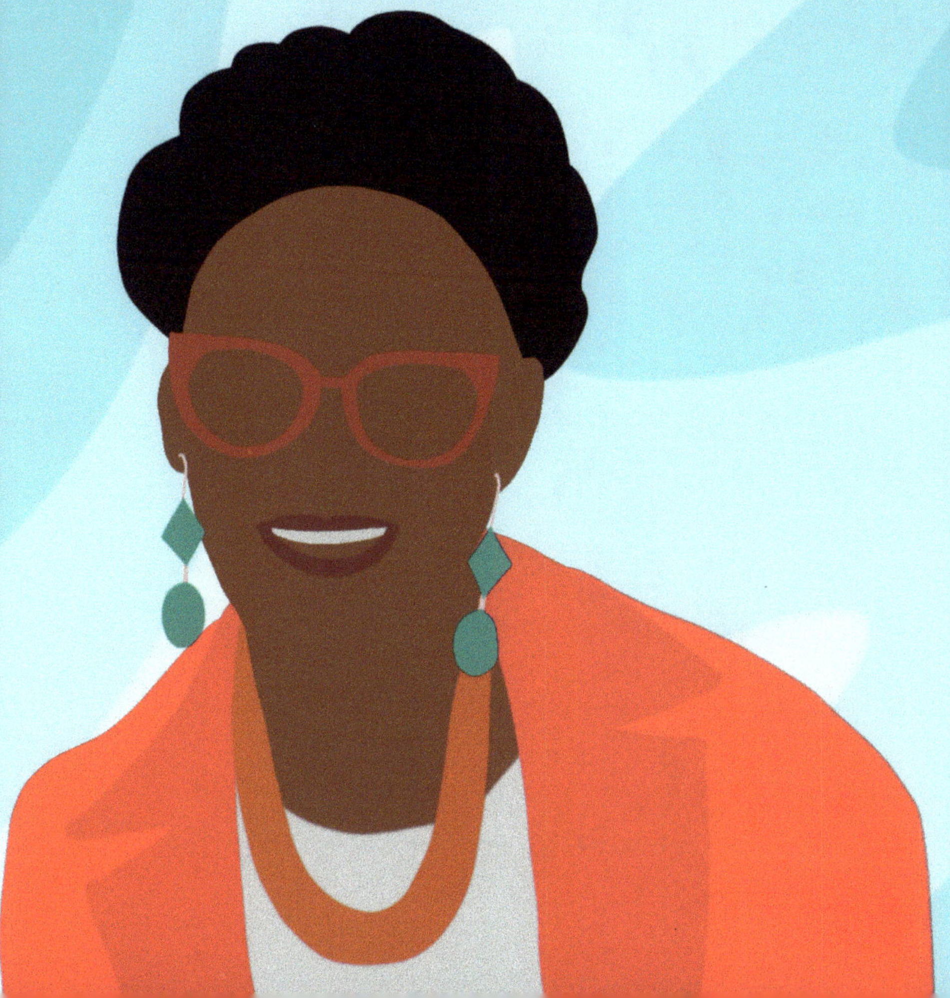

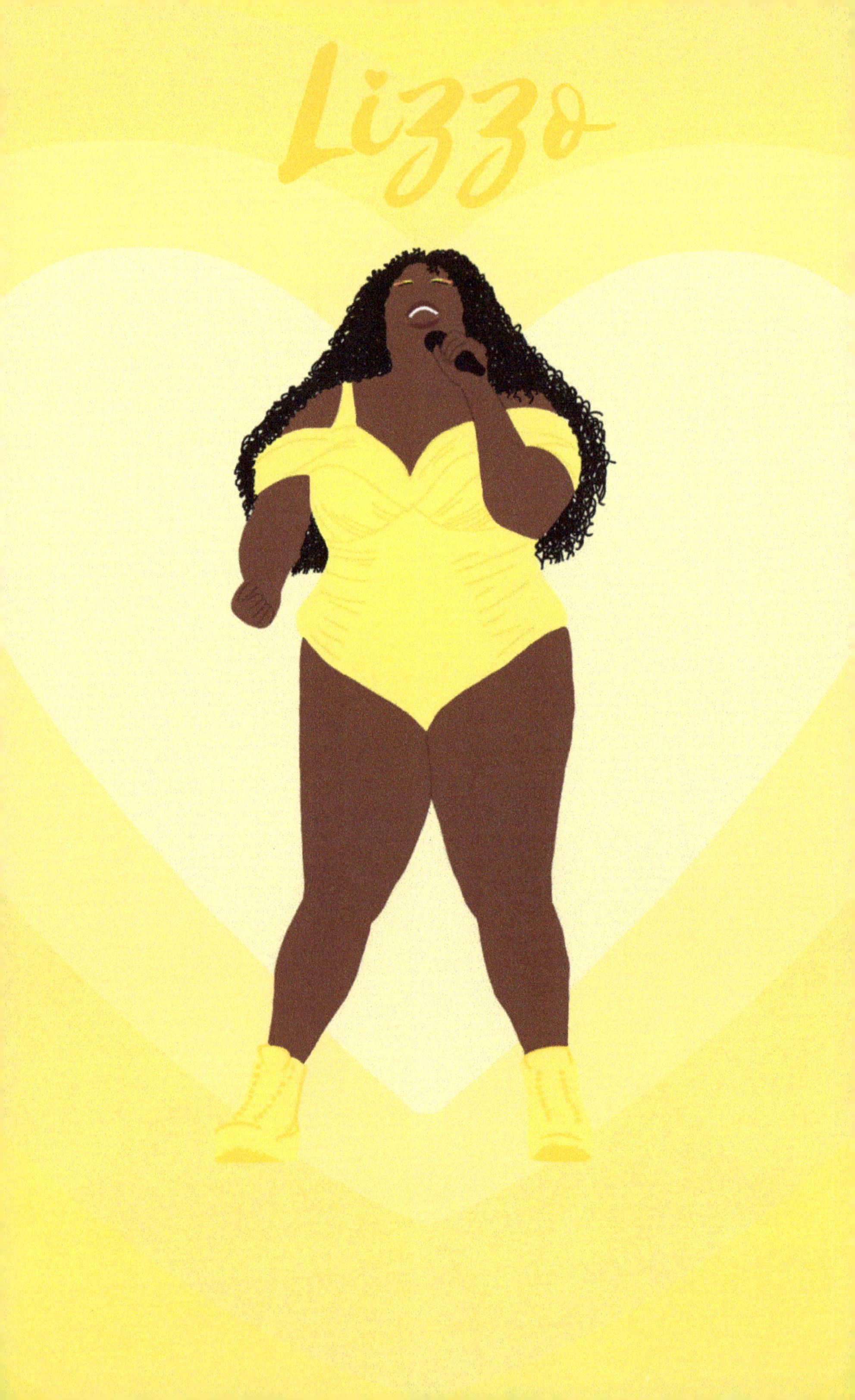
Lizzo

Melissa Viviane Jefferson, better known by her stage name Lizzo, was born in Detroit in 1988. Her passion for music blossomed when she was just 10 years old, as she classically trained in the flute. In addition to continuing her classical training throughout her teenage years, she also added marching band and rapping to her musical repertoire. Jefferson started her band, Cornrow Clique, and adopted the alias "Lizzo" when she was 14. After graduating high school in 2006, she pursued further education in classical music and flute at the University of Houston. Within a year of her father's death when she was 20 years old, Lizzo was living in her car and attempting to launch a career in music. Her debut album, *Lizzobangers*, quickly gained attention following its release and led to Lizzo touring the United States and United Kingdom. The road to her commercial breakthrough began with her signing with Atlantic Records and being recognized by *Rolling Stone* and *Time* magazine.

In addition to her contributions to the alternative and hip hop music industries, Lizzo is well known for her advocacy of body positivity and self-love. These themes, along with queerness, blackness, and individuality are reflected in her music. Facing struggles with her personal body image as a plus-sized woman, she has taken steps to help other young girls love their bodies just as she does hers. The backup dancers in her performances are all plus-sized, and Lizzo herself has been featured in runway shows and on the cover of the October 2020 issue of *Vogue*. In fact, she has been credited as redefining the "body-positivity" movement to "body-neutrality." This movement challenges the idea that one has to necessarily celebrate their fat body, instead suggesting that bodies be regarded as functional, neutral parts rather than something that must adhere to a beauty standard. She uses her platform to educate about healthy living for the sake of *feeling* good rather than looking good and to advocate for the enjoyment of one's body rather than trying to change it. Her tireless dedication to this movement has inspired millions of young women to appreciate their appearance as it is.

Yayoi Kusama was born in 1929 in Matsumoto, Japan as the youngest daughter in her family. Her interest in painting was apparent at an early age, as she developed her unique painting style of her own volition. Despite her parents' discouragement of her career interest, instead favoring a more traditional house role for herself, Kusama persisted on her own path. Inspiration for her signature arrays of polka dots came from symptoms of her dissociative disorder. Suffering from hallucinations associated with depersonalization-derealization disorder, young Kusama depicted her dotted visions in her art. She finally attended the Kyoto City Specialist School of Arts when she was 19 years old. By organizing exhibitions across Japan, Kusama was able to break away from her conservative upbringing and societal pressure to prove her talent and worth as an artist. In order to bolster her artistic career, Kusama moved to New York City and created a variety of exploratory and groundbreaking paintings. Her art, which was known for providing an experience for its viewers, put her at the front of the avant-garde movement. Transitioning into sculpting and performance art, Kusama adopted political and mental health themes in her work. At the height of American involvement in the Vietnam War, her work presented anti-war and anti-violent sentiments through symbolism. After moving back to Japan in 1973, Kusama had an extended stay in a psychiatric ward, where she continued to express herself through the arts. She wrote poetry and fiction, further exploring themes present in the performance art she debuted after her move to New York.

Kusama made her return to the art scene in 1989, beginning with shows in New York City and England. This was followed by installations she set in Venice, Los Angeles, Tokyo, and Washington, D.C. In a culmination of her impressive career, Kusama launched the Yayoi Kusama Museum in Tokyo, adjacent to her studio and previous psychiatric ward. By overcoming societal pressure and pursuing her passion, Kusama was able to use her talent to bring attention to social issues through the universal language of art.

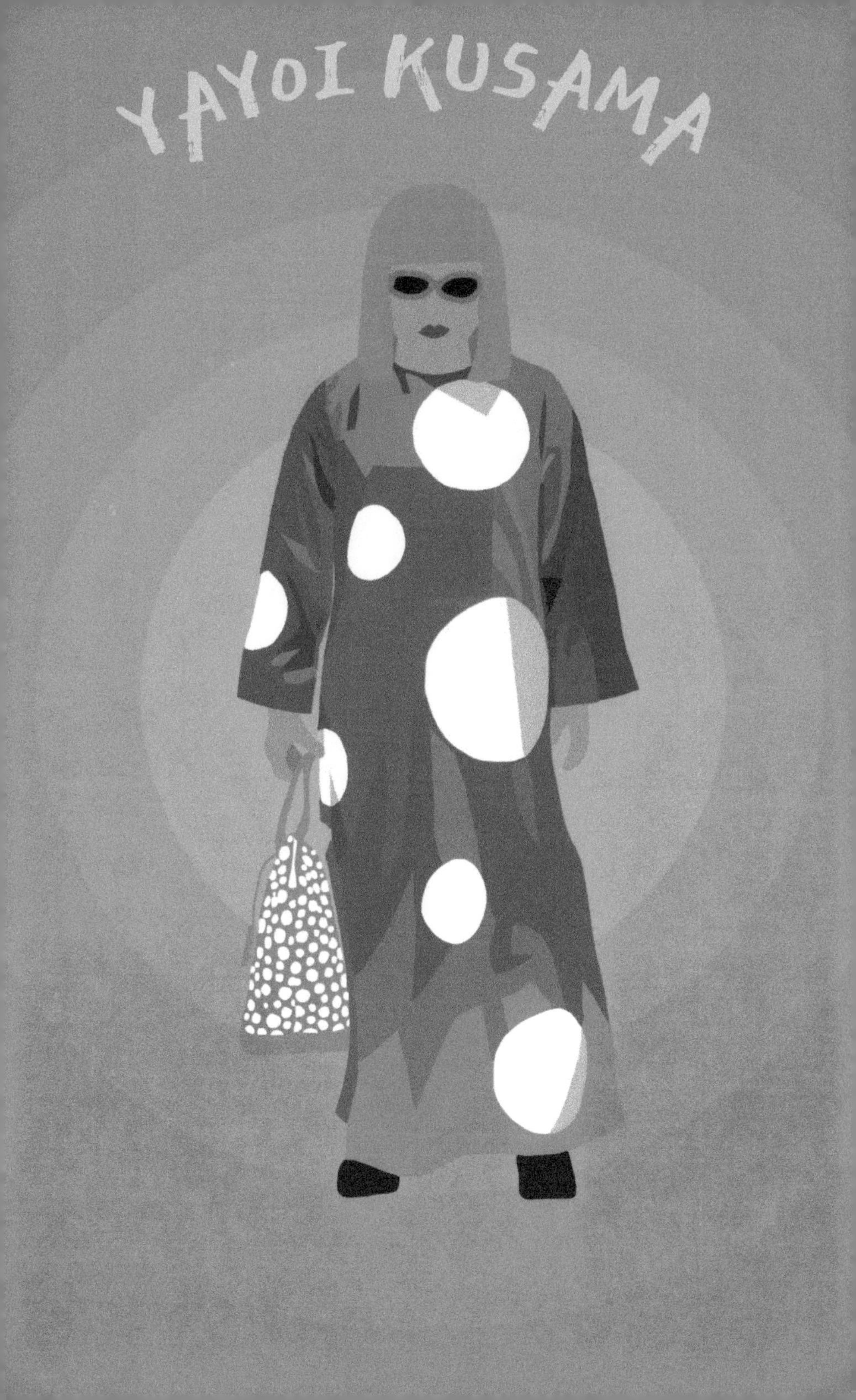
YAYOI KUSAMA

PART 5:

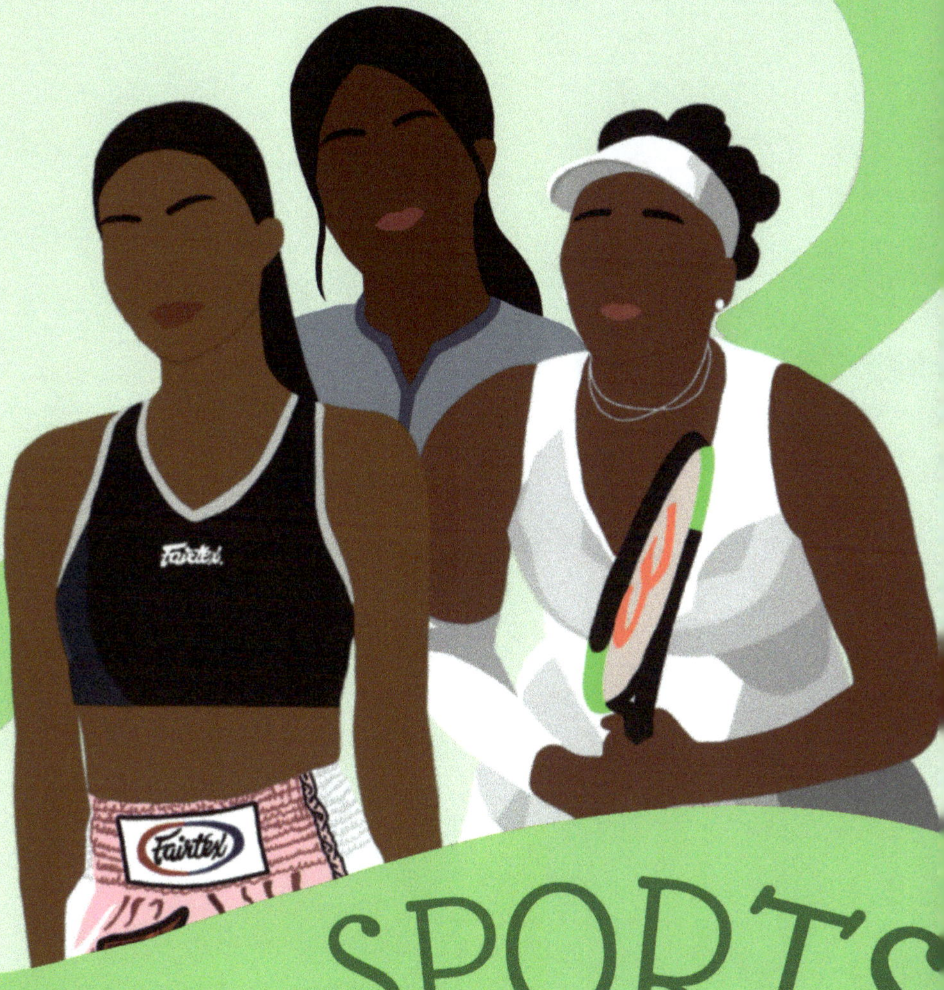

SPORTS

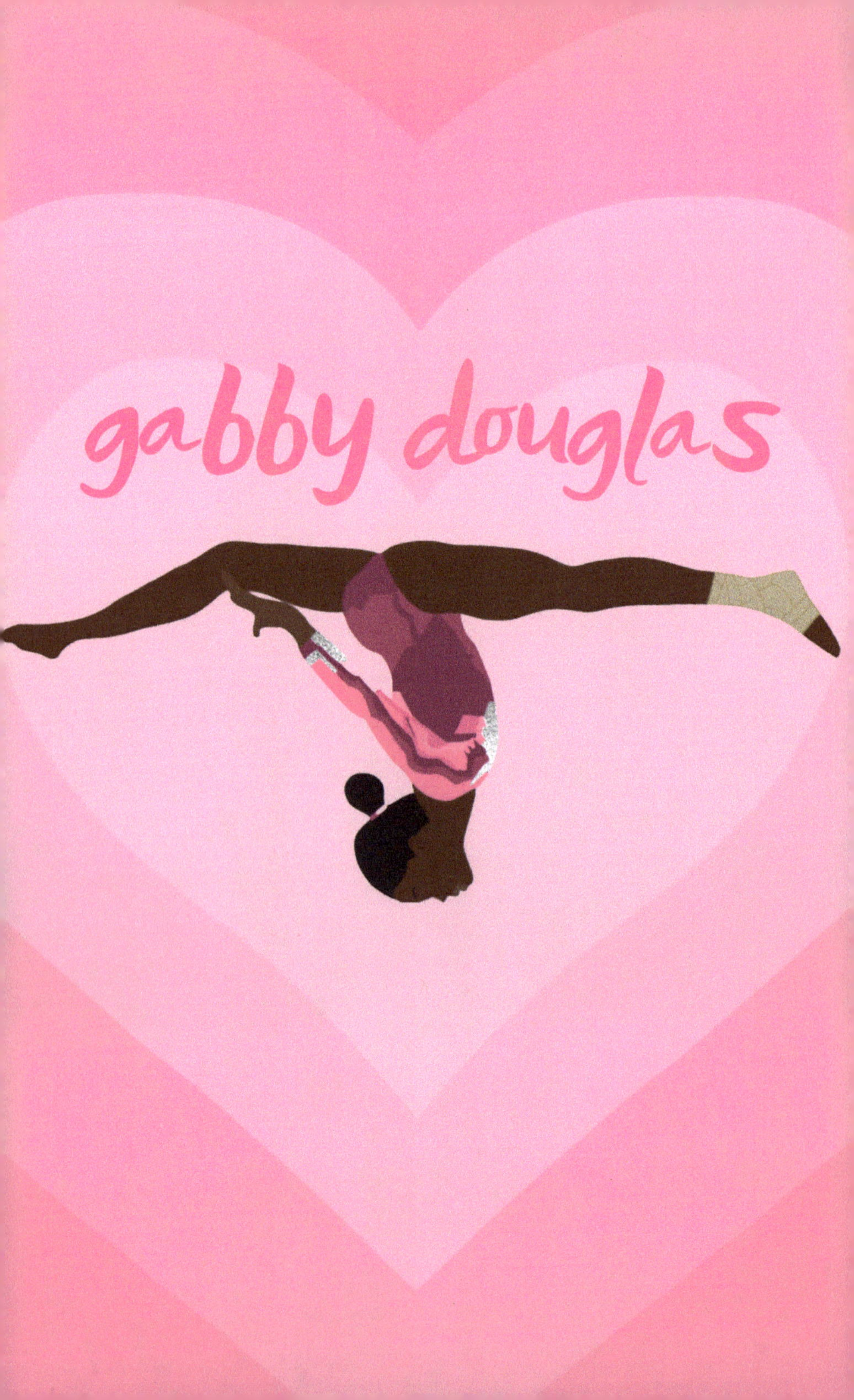
gabby douglas

Olympic gymnast Gabrielle Douglas was born on December 31, 1995 in Virginia. She grew up in Virginia Beach with her parents and three older siblings. Douglas began training in gymnastics when she was just six years old and immediately showed promise as a talented athlete. By 8 years of age, she had won a title at the Virginia State Championship and began training full-time at 14 years of age. Douglas went on to compete in the 2012 Summer Olympics when she was 16, bringing home two gold medals. She spent her remaining teenage years training for and competing in international competitions.

Aside from being an incredibly accomplished athlete, Douglas is known for her activism within the gymnastics community. The esteemed athlete made history, being the first Black female gymnast to win an all-around Olympic gold medal. By overcoming societal barriers related to her gender and race, she inspired many young Black girls to excel as she did. She has faced criticism for competing in her natural hair, which was condemned for being "unkempt." Many social media users came to Douglas' defense, as natural hair can be a significant aspect of a Black woman's identity. Despite the pressure that she received in 2012 to straighten her hair, Douglas returned to the 2016 Olympics proudly winning a gold medal and sporting her beautiful, textured hair.

Venus Ebony Starr Williams was born on June 17, 1980, in Lynwood, California. She picked up a tennis racquet before even starting kindergarten, and her talent for tennis became apparent from the start of her training. Local tennis player Tony Chesta was quick to realize her potential. Just three years later, her whole family moved from Compton, California, to Florida so that she could attend an elite tennis academy. Here, both Williams and her sister Serena received rigorous coaching from Rick Macci, another former professional tennis player. As the tennis prodigies became increasingly dedicated to the sport, their father Richard felt that they needed a more balanced lifestyle. One year into training with Macci, Richard barred them from attending national tennis tournaments to allow them more time to focus on school. He also loathed the racist and derogatory comments that other parents had made regarding his children in competitions. Despite these discouraging comments, Williams had not yet lost a single match in her career, placing her at the top of national and state charts. In 1995, she left the official training academy to be coached by her father.

Williams' thorough training and incredible talent translated into success in her career. Her aggressive playing style and versatile skill brought her to her debut at the US Open in 1997, where she reached the semifinals. Slowly rising through the ranks of the world's best tennis players, she placed within the top 10 for multiple consecutive years. However, her career was not without injury and illness. After multiple injuries and unexplained symptoms, she was diagnosed with Sjorgen's syndrome. The autoimmune disorder would impact her muscle and joint health, preventing Williams from playing to her full potential. Amazingly, following a short break following her diagnosis, Williams fought through her illness to attain national titles and three Olympic gold medals!

Williams is known for her philanthropy, donating to myriad non-profit organizations and supporting them publicly. She also speaks out about her diagnosis and how it has affected her playing, inspiring others with the same illness and other afflictions. Her record has sparked an interest in tennis in many young boys and girls, especially as Black women are underrepresented in the sport. With her continued success, it is clear why Venus Williams is often referred to as one of the greatest tennis players of all time.

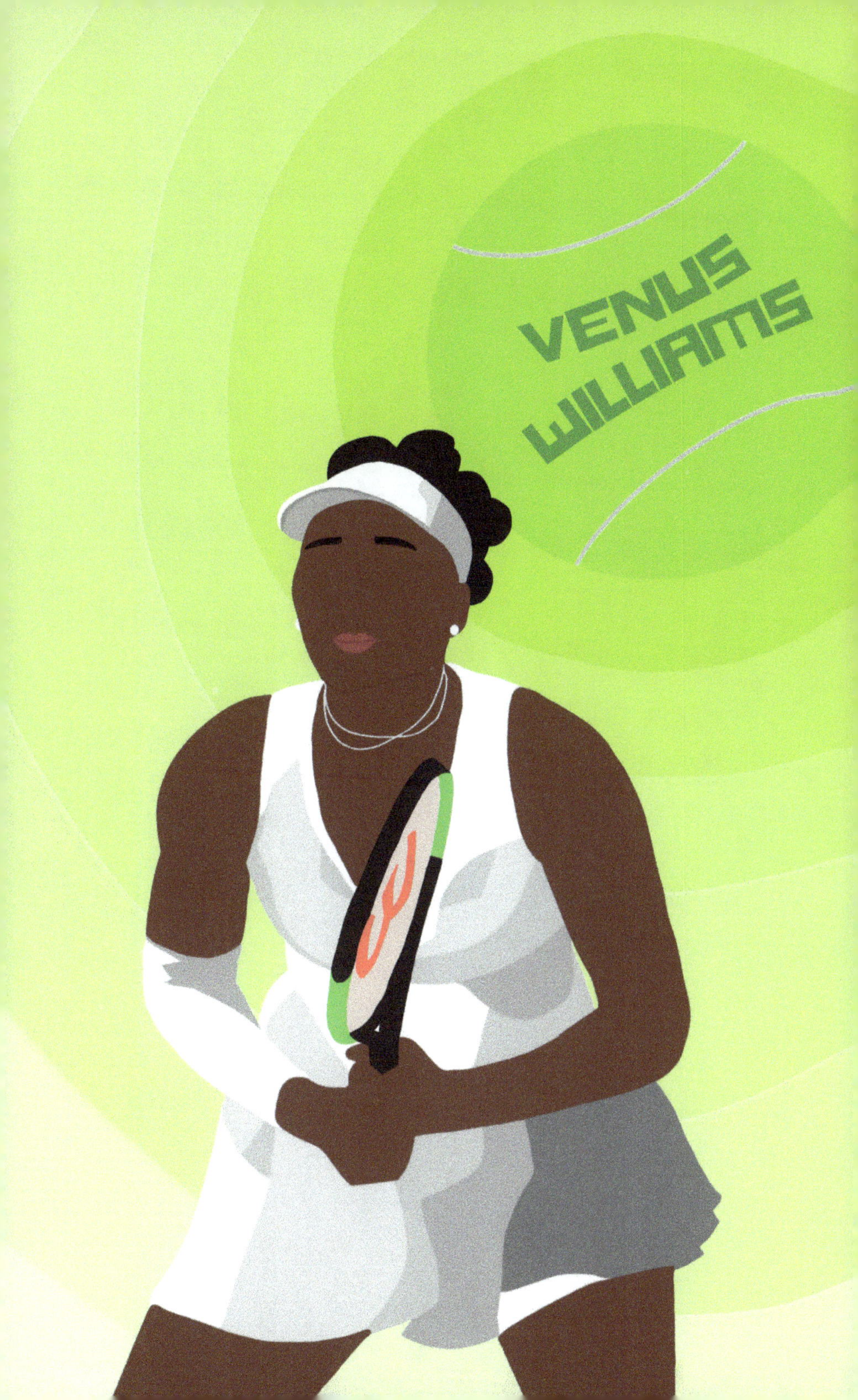
VENUS
WILLIAMS

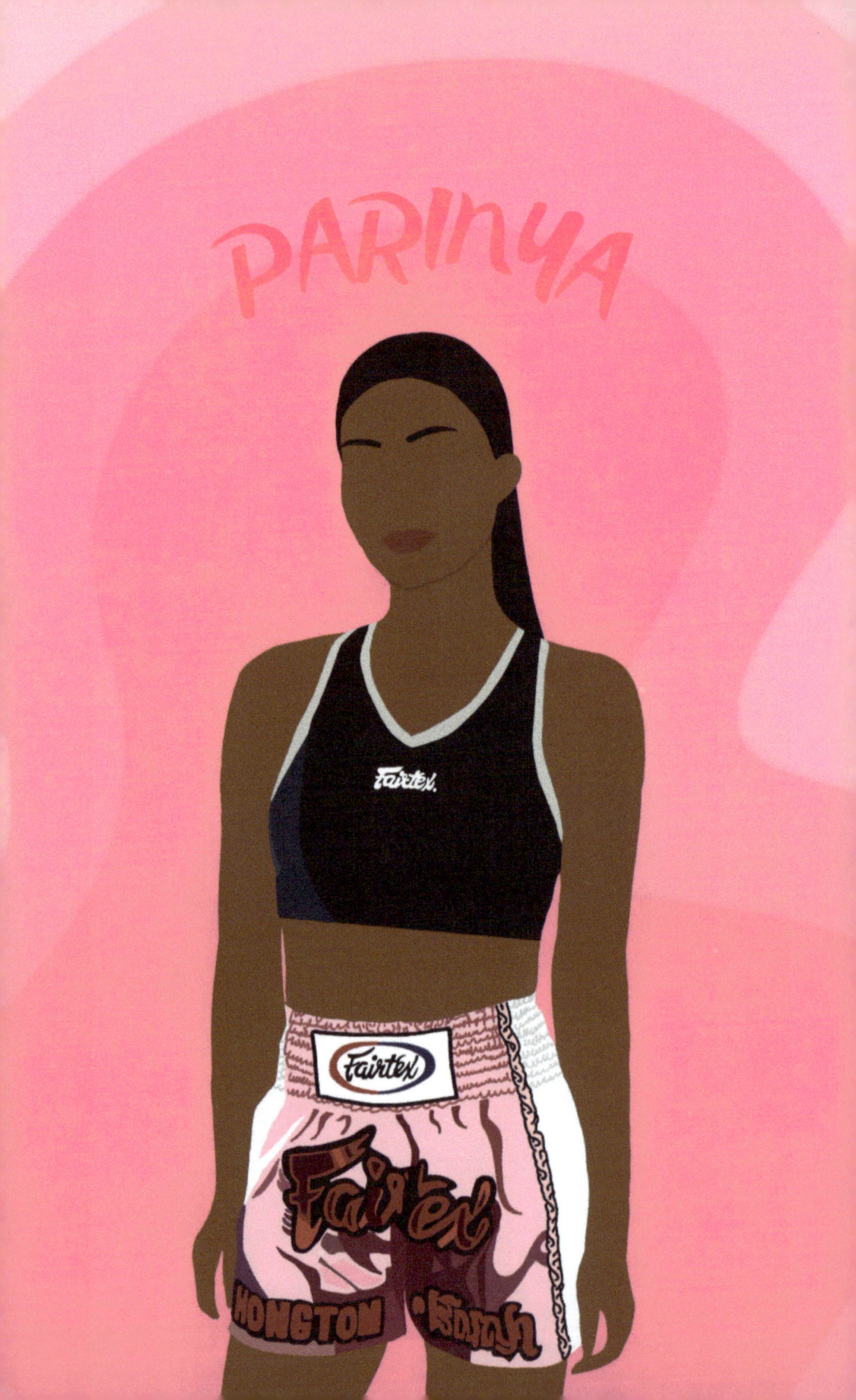
PARINYA
Fairtex
Fairtex
Fairtex
HONGTON

Parinya Charoenphol was born in 1981 in Thailand. Knowing that she identified with the female gender, despite being born biologically male, she was known as a *kathoey*, or a transgender girl. After some time living as a Buddhist monk, Charoenphol began martial arts training in hopes of bringing her parents out of poverty and funding her surgical transition. With training from a Muay Thai camp, she competed in Bangkok's Lumpini Boxing Stadium at just 16 years of age. Her victory-- as a young, effeminate *kathoey*-- in this competition intrigued audiences worldwide. Media channels, magazines, and music video directors flocked to this martial arts sensation to sign her for appearances. Under her stage name Nong Toom, Charoenphol collected win after win, ending her boxing career in 1999 with a total of 20 victories and 18 knockouts. That same year, she finally underwent the gender-confirmation surgery, which she had yearned for all along, at Yanhee International Hospital.

Opening a new chapter in her life, Charoenphol took to singing, acting, and modeling. In 2003, the biographical film *Beautiful Boxer* was released, exploring the challenges she faced throughout her life. The director of this award-winning film invited Charoenphol to star in a theatre performance, *Boxing Cabaret*. She performed in Bangkok, the Singapore Arts Festival, and theaters around the United States. Charoenphol, also, briefly returned to the boxing scene, competing in exhibitions against Japanese, Swedish, and Dutch boxers. After moving back to Thailand, she discovered that her homeland would no longer allow her to compete because of her gender identity. In 2010, she retired and opened her boxing camp, Parinya Muay Thai, in Thailand. Despite the discrimination that her gender identity has caused her, Charoenphol has proven to be incredibly talented and tenacious. Achieving her dreams as a successful boxer and fully-transitioned woman, despite a poverty-stricken past and societal backlash, she truly has earned the attention and praise she has attained.

ACKNOWLEDGEMENTS

Firstly, I want to thank my parents, who were especially supportive of me during my writing journey. I would be nowhere without their constant encouragement and motivation, and for that I can't thank them enough. I can't begin to express my gratitude towards my sister, Monica, who has had my back since we were babies. She is the strongest and most caring person I know, and I couldn't ask for a better sister. I am so fortunate to have the Muthuraj family by my side.

Special thanks to Ayra, Aysha, and Dhruvi, my best friends and found family. Thank you for listening to my excited rants about this project, and for getting excited with me.

I must recognize the people who gave me the idea to take on this project in the first place-- Shiv and Janini. Your ideas and support were invaluable throughout the writing process. Of course, I have to thank the diligent team of researchers who found the beauty in the lives of these women. Suneeta, Samantha, Maria, and Sarah-Jean-- you guys were truly the heart of this project. Finally, this book wouldn't have made it past its first draft if it wasn't for Mrs. Kushinsky, my amazing and incredibly dedicated editor. Thank you all for your crucial roles in the creation of *The Power of Venus*.

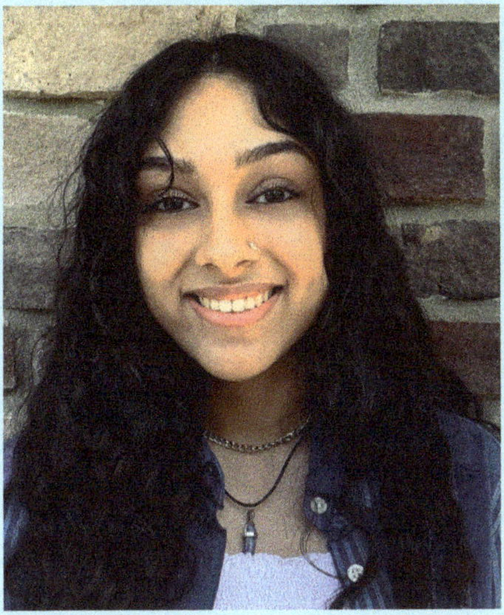

Sonia Muthuraj is a 17-year-old, born and raised in Edison, New Jersey. While *The Power of Venus* is her debut novel, her love of writing dates back to her childhood when she spent lazy snow days writing short stories. In addition to writing, she has always been incredibly passionate about psychology and feminism.

Notorious for her "bad habit" of obsessing over every new book she reads, especially if it has a strong female lead, Sonia felt it right that her next project should be a book highlighting strong women—one that she herself would obsess over.

CPSIA information can be obtained
at www.ICGtesting.com
Printed in the USA
LVHW050154221021
701073LV00008B/31

9 781637 651117